It's A Cat's Life

also by the authors
The Natural Cat

IT'S A CAT'S LIFE

*True Stories with Practical Help
for Your Cat
from Birth to Old Age*

Anitra Frazier
with Norma Eckroate

Illustrations by Cris Arbo
and James Francis Yax

BEAUFORT BOOKS *Publishers* • NEW YORK

Library of Congress Cataloging–in–Publication Data

Frazier, Anitra, 1936–
  It's a cat's life.

  1. Cats.   2. Cats—Diseases.   3. Cats—Anecdotes.
I. Eckroate, Norma, 1951– . II. Title.
SF447.F69 1985   636.8   85-9143
ISBN 0-8253-0302-8

Published in the United States by Beaufort Books Publishers, New York.

Designer: Christine Swirnoff / Libra Graphics, Inc.

Printed in the U.S.A.   First Edition

10 9 8 7 6 5 4 3 2 1

ACKNOWLEDGMENTS

I would like to express my heartfelt thanks to:

Gina Cerminara, Valerie Coates, Phyllis Embleton, Robert Gottlieb, David Guinn, Dr. Gerald Johnson, Eric Kampmann, Lucy Kaplan, Phyllis Levy, Lombardi's Restaurant, Susan Suffes and Integral Yoga Institute.

All my clients who have given such cheerful cooperation when I've had to reschedule appointments because of a pussycat emergency;

The secret sponsors who have supported so many cats in need through treatments and therapies;

And, above all, to Big Purr, my cat-in-chief, for his unfailing support of me and his judicious management of our Feline Health Spa.

A.F.

I dedicate my work on this book to:
> Paul Solomon, who has taught me to
> more fully express joy and unconditional
> love in all that I do;
> > and
> All who are working to reestablish the
> balance between man and the animal and
> plant kingdoms and the Divine
> connection that links us all together.
>
> N.E.

Chapter Dedications
> Chapter 1: *For Dorothea Kulp*
> Chapter 2: *For Ursula Jahoda*
> Chapter 3: *For Olga Aparicio*
> Chapter 4: *For Dr. Richard Pitcairn*
> Chapter 5: *For Marcey Lindheimer*
> Chapter 6: *For my Mother, Charlotte G.*
> *Pierson*

Contents

AUTHORS' NOTES

The incidents related in this book are all true. However, the identities of the cats and the people involved have been disguised for obvious reasons.

This book is based on a holistic approach to cat care. In order to allow for continuity in the stories, specific information on care has been included in the Appendices, at the end of the book. Diets and supplements are given in Appendix A; information on giving medications and nutritional supplements is found in Appendix B; and product suppliers are listed in Appendix C.

SU-SHI'S STORY

CHAPTER ONE

Su-Shi's Story
Pregnancy and Birth

"Know anybody who wants a cat?" That's how it started, with a phone call from Alma Malloy, owner of the Ming-Loy Cattery.

Big Alma was never the type to give away cats; she was a woman who liked her profits. So, when she told me that the cat in question was none other than Triple Champion Thompson's Su-Shi of Ming-Loy, I was eager to learn the rest of the story.

"She's a beautiful cat," Alma went on, "that's not the problem. If I wanted to keep on showing her she'd take every ribbon in the place, but she throws bad kittens."

When a queen, or female cat, gives birth, she "throws" a litter. Alma's comment meant that Su-Shi gave birth to kittens that were not of show quality. Su-Shi's kittens were considered "pet types": hearty little throwbacks that did not have the physical attributes necessary to win ribbons. Alma had tried breeding Su-

Shi several times to several different males, but the results were always the same: Her kittens' eyes were round, instead of the required almond shape, and their heads were shaped like those of any domestic cat, instead of tapering to the required aristocratic wedge. And, she threw small litters of only two or three kittens, which was hardly profitable for a big cattery like Ming-Loy.

So, when Alma finally came to the point of her call, I was not too surprised. "Now she's pregnant again," she grumbled. "I can't keep throwing good money after bad. I thought you might know somebody who'd take her off my hands."

It was fairly obvious what she really had in mind. She wanted me to be that somebody.

I pretended not to take the bait. "I can't think of a soul right off, Alma, but I'll certainly put the word out and we'll see what I can come up with for you."

Alma muttered her thanks and rang off. I was thoroughly intrigued and I sat at my desk for a minute, letting the information sink in. Some puny, inbred show cat wasn't making the money she was supposed to make and Big Alma wanted her out of there. I wondered what Triple Champion Thompson's Su-Shi of Ming-Loy was really like. Siamese are bred to be tiny; her name was probably a lot bigger than she was. I knew she was a breeding queen and that she was five years old.

Like all show cats, her name told me her history. Su-Shi was her given name, the name she was called by. The possessive "Thompson's" before it meant that she had been born at Jeff Thompson's cattery. "Ming-Loy" indicated that Ming-Loy Cattery, in the person of Alma Malloy, had bought and shown her. "Triple Champion" meant that, as Alma had said, she was winning every ribbon in sight, but what good was that if her kittens didn't look like winners, too?

The only reason for going to the trouble and expense of showing a cat and winning a lot of ribbons is so that the cattery will be able to demand a high price for her kittens. But as a breeding queen, Triple Champion Su-Shi of Ming-Loy was a failure.

Back in those days, I was still accepting an occasional role in summer stock, so I traveled. I had no cats of my own, nor was I planning on acquiring any. Still, the poor thing was in a precarious position. I needed more information and, since I'd learned as much as I was likely to learn from Alma, I decided to put in a friendly call to Jeff Thompson, who bred this little problem cat in the first place. Jeff, an easygoing, garrulous sort, was happy to fill me in on her early life.

Su-Shi had been pampered and petted from the day she was born. Su-Shi's mother, Patti-Paws, had been pampered and petted before her; life was like that at the Thompson cattery. Patti-Paws, Jeff's top breeding queen, was famous throughout Siamese breeding circles for the high quality of her very large litters.

Baby Su-Shi arrived with Patti Paw's fifth litter, an event awaited with high hopes and great expectations by Mr. Thompson, for the sire had been none other than Grand Champion Ming-Loy's Samurai the Third, owned by, you guessed it, Alma Malloy. Samurai's picture had appeared on the cover of the two leading cat magazines and his stud fee was well into the four-figure category. When Jeff Thompson announced his intention to join the two bloodlines of Patti Paws and

Samurai, the waiting list of prospective kitten buyers was filled and closed long before the actual mating took place. As was the custom, the asking price for one kitten would be about the same as the stud fee.

Baby Su-Shi, of course, knew nothing of all this. She knew only that her world was warm and pleasant. She reveled in the gentle nurturing of the sweet and motherly Patti Paws and passed her first three weeks in a trusting haze of bliss. Life was good and the world was a fine place. She naturally assumed that it would continue that way.

Periodically the gigantic form of old Mr. Thompson would loom over the breeding cage and mama Patti Paws would rub her cheek against the wire door and purr. Often he would open the door and baby Su-Shi would watch his big hand reach into the cage to lift Patti Paws high into the air and hold her close against his cheek. Then Patti Paws would smile and purr in a voice quite different from the one she used with her kittens.

One day, after Su-Shi was about three weeks old, Mr. Thompson's big hand reached in and Su-Shi was scooped up into the air and set down on his lap close beside her mother. Then he began to stroke her with one big rough finger. She felt him gently smooth the fur down the side of her neck and stroke lightly under her chest and then along her back. And Su-Shi found out why her mother always smiled and purred whenever Mr. Thompson came by.

Jeff Thompson was a big kindly old man. He was in the business of raising Siamese because he loved them. Jeff knew what life on the show circuit required of a cat, so, beginning at the age of three weeks, each little aristocrat was gently prepared. They were thoroughly handled, stroked and stretched, poked and prodded, and lifted and turned in all the ways that a cat show judge might do. They were trundled about in carriers and bedded down in all manner of cages. Jeff took pride in seeing to it that any kittens out of Thompson Cattery would fit right into the life they were expected to lead.

Su-Shi and her litter mates knew no other life and so they casually accepted it all and simply assumed that this was the way all cats lived. Besides, it felt good to be handled and admired. Life was good, and the world was still a fine place. What Su-Shi didn't know was that at the end of her eighth week her life was going to change completely.

Months before, when Jeff had arranged for Ming-Loy's Samurai the Third to sire Patti Paws' fifth litter, he had made the usual deal—Alma would have the right to either her large stud fee or pick of the litter.

Jeff assumed that Alma would follow her usual routine. She always came by to examine the litter when they were about seven weeks old, then she always took the stud fee instead of a kitten.

"Ming-Loy Cattery already has the best," she would remark, "what do I want with somebody else's kitten?" Alma was known for her business sense, if not for her tact.

Mr. Thompson, who had grown rather fond of his little beauties, fervently hoped that Alma would again take her stud fee and go away.

But Alma Malloy was no fool. When she saw baby Su-Shi romping in the big breeding cage with the other little kittens, she didn't hestiate a minute. Pointing a bejeweled finger, "I'll take that one," she announced.

And so, at the age of eight weeks, Su-Shi was

whisked away to follow in her father's footsteps, bringing ribbons and renown to Alma Malloy and the Ming-Loy Cattery. And that's exactly what she did. Su-Shi was a triple champion before she was three.

When I confided to Jeff the reason behind my inquiries, he was distressed to hear of Su-Shi's predicament, amazed that her career had taken this odd turn, and concerned about how it might reflect on the Thompson Cattery. He made it clear that he would be enormously relieved if she could be settled safely and quietly with me.

I made no promises but gave my word to keep him posted on any further developments. I sat for a while, thinking over the situation. It was ironic that I, the advocate of neutering and spaying, the lover of the strong and healthy mixed-breed cat, should be offered a delicate, inbred triple-champion Siamese, and a pregnant one at that. The thought of owning such a cat was ridiculous. Anyway, I traveled; but then, so do show cats, and if she was small. . . . Well, it certainly couldn't hurt to look into the situation a little further. I made up my mind to brave the rigors of the New York subway and go up to the Bronx to have a look.

Emerging from the netherworld of the subway, I found myself in a gentle neighborhood of row houses, clipped hedges, and small-fry on tricycles. It was a relaxing three-block walk to the Ming-Loy Cattery.

Alma Malloy showed me into a rather overstuffed living room which was literally festooned with lounging Siamese cats. She pointed out Su-Shi to me—sitting with two other show types among the sofa cushions, busily enjoying the ritual of mutual grooming. The world was obviously still a fine place as far as Su-Shi was concerned; she had no reason to doubt that life would go on just as it was. She had not the slightest inkling that she was about to be pitched out of her happy home.

"Su-Shi!" her owner barked, as if she were breaking up a dog fight.

Su-Shi turned her head and gracefully extricated her body from the warmth of her friends. She stretched sinuously, gave a little yawn, and leaped off the couch. She was grace incarnate. Her leap flowed in slow motion, as if she were swimming through air. She was the slimmest cat I had ever seen. Siamese are bred to be thin and long; that's the fashion in Siamese. Well, Su-Shi was not a triple champion for nothing. Her tiny wedge-shaped head was surmounted by two enormous ears, now pricked forward in happy expectation. The chocolate brown mask and ears matched her long, long stockings and whiplike tail. Her body was a milky fawn color. Indeed, she was a perfect chocolate point Siamese. She minced her way over to us, quacking a Siamese question, turned her back, and sat down directly at my feet. Show cats are always turned around to face away when the judge lifts them out of their cage. By turning her back to me, Su-Shi was politely presenting her charming triple champion self to be picked up and admired at close range. She was purring in a most unaristocratic manner. I soon discovered that Su-Shi would begin purring the minute anyone walked into the room, because she naturally assumed that she was about to be picked up.

"The veterinarian's coming Friday to give shots," Alma frowned, as Su-Shi continued the mutual grooming on my chin. "I suppose if she's still here by then,

I'll just have him put her to sleep. I can't keep throwing good money after bad."

"I'll take her," I said.

And so, Triple Champion Thompson's Su-Shi of Ming-Loy came home to live with me.

Given my strong opinion against bringing more cats into the world, you may well ask why I didn't immediately have her aborted and spayed. I considered it, believe me. I've advised it many a time, before and since. I'm a firm believer in the slogan of the Pet Pride organization: "Neuter and spay, it's the kindest way."

There are not enough homes for the cats already alive in the world. Last year, in one major city, one public animal shelter alone had to put 24,000 cats and kittens to sleep because there was just no room for them. These were not only "diseased strays." No indeed! Shelters regularly have to kill Persians, Siamese, and kittens, as well as hundreds of healthy mixed breed family pets. Even if everyone who decided to get a cat went out right now and adopted one from a public shelter, there would *still* be a terrible surplus—and surplus items become cheap. They are not respected.

In light of this, I will never understand how anyone can breed more cats. When a professional breeder starts talking about "preserving the typical qualities of the breed," I have to point out that the "typical qualities of the breed" disappeared long ago when breeders started using in-breeding to bring out the very *untyp*-ical, recessive traits of the breed. The pitiful flat face of the Persian, called a peke face (as in Pekinese), is not a "quality of the breed" but a congenital deformity. The malformed tear ducts that usually result produce the runny eyes so often seen in pure-bred Persians today. The straight nose and wedge-shaped head of the modern Siamese cat is another example of in-breeding to achieve an extreme and exaggerated look without any regard for the health of the animal. The original Siamese did not have this extreme head shape.

For years I have been advising owners of the ideal time for neutering and spaying—after the female's first heat or, for a male, after the urine begins to smell very strong and pungent. These are the signs that maturity has been achieved and the sexual center has transferred from the sexual organs to the base of the brain. The organs can then be removed without in any way interfering with the basic sexuality of the cat.

Neutered males and spayed females live longer, healthier lives than unneutered and unspayed cats. If a male is not neutered, he fights. If he fights, he will receive puncture wounds and sooner or later one will become infected and cause serious illness or death. Unneutered males on the loose die young—usually from infected wounds.

In the case of females, the reasons are twofold. First, although the eggs are ready when a female comes into heat, she does not release and pass them off as humans do. If fertilization does not occur cysts are formed around the unfertilized eggs and they are retained. Cystic ovaries in unspayed females that are not bred regularly are the rule, not the exception. Secondly, although most females mate and breed without injury, owners should be aware that there is a very high risk factor involved. Mating can be a rough and violent ritual. Unspayed females sometimes receive spinal injuries when the male bites the neck to mount them. Many more die during delivery, especially small cats and Persians who are purposely bred to have small pelvic bones. I once saw six different cats brought into one veterinarian's office in one day for emergency caesarean sections.

My decision not to have Su-Shi aborted was based on two facts. First, she was three and a half weeks pregnant, one-third of the way into her term. Her glands were programmed for pregnancy, and, because she was such an inbred, delicate little thing, I judged it better not to interrupt the cycle. The second and biggest factor which influenced my decision to let Nature take its course was the fact that Su-Shi always threw small litters. After all, she was notorious for it. I hoped that this time again, she would have only two kittens.

In all my studies of cat care, I had only skimmed through the care and feeding of pregnant and lactating queens, since I never expected to have much use for knowledge about something of which I disapproved so strongly. Now I pulled out all the old reference books on pregnancy and lactation and began avidly devouring everything from *Let's Have Healthy Children*, by Adelle Davis, to a treatise on piometria (uterine infection) in English Bull Terriers. If I was going to be party to bringing innocent kittens into this crowded world, the least I could do was to do it well and learn all I could from the experience.

As soon as I got her home I made an appointment for old Dr. Van Kluff to give Su-Shi a once-over. I advise all my clients to take any new cat right to their own veterinarian. No matter where you get the cat or what the attending veterinarian has told you, I have found that it always pays to have a second, trusted opinion, especially if you have another cat at home. In that case, I advise taking the new cat to your own veterinarian *before* bringing him home. Then any problem can be treated and cleared up right away, without the possibility of infecting your other cat.

The carrying case was vibrating with Su-Shi's melodious purr as I set it down on the examining room floor. The purr began to build when I opened the case, and reached full volume as I lifted Su-Shi out and placed her on the cold metal table. As Dr. Van Kluff reached for her, Su-Shi turned around, and politely presented her back.

"Vell, vell, so ve have a real little lady here, eh?" Dr. Van Kluff's old-world accent was subtle and quite charming. "And she is, as you say, in the delicate condition, yes?"

Su-Shi wore her look of happy expectation as the doctor's big hands stroked down her body. Her eyes blinked half-closed with pleasure as he began palpating her abdomen, checking out her internal organs. She looked even more delicate and tiny in the hands of the big doctor, with his bushy gray hair and beard and the heavy black-rimmed spectacles, which perched precariously and slid frequently down the long slope of his enormous aquiline nose. He wore that faraway look he always got when he was feeling with his fingers or listening through the stethoscope.

"She is terribly inbred," I began. "She's been used as a breeding queen for two years, but she's so tiny and delicate I want to be very sure she's not going to have any difficulty giving birth this time. I'd like to be sure her blood count is okay too."

Dr. Van Kluff smiled patiently and asked when she

had been bred. He was always smiling patiently. It was part and parcel of his marvelously reassuring image.

He must have had some training in psychology, for he knew that if you want to keep the cat calm, you have to keep the owner calm. I did observe, however, that one could always tell when he thought a situation was getting out of hand, because that very charming old-world accent would begin to thicken perceptibly.

"They bred her four weeks ago," I replied, holding Su-Shi by the shoulders as the doctor took her foreleg to draw a blood sample.

"Vell, vell, five veeks to go, eh?"

Su-Shi was daintly washing the doctor's thumb as he inserted the needle.

"You can give me a call during the last week, before the kittens are coming and I vill take a look at her and see how she is doing." He removed the hypodermic. "I vill have the blood results for you in a couple of days," he said. And that was that!

Su-Shi herself displayed the same equanimity and calm about the situation as the doctor. So I did the worrying for all three of us over the coming weeks. I couldn't help it. She was so tiny, so delicate, my dainty aristocrat.

Su-Shi settled right down to her new life in my apartment. She soon discovered that the old grooming ritual she loved so much could still be enjoyed every night when I lay down in bed. I had the cleanest chin in town.

She accepted such lifestyle changes as sleeping on my pillow curled against my cheek, instead of in a cage, and lounging on my lap, instead of gadding about from show to show, as no more than a normal progression of events. After all, she had already established in her mind that the world was a fine place, so she was not in the least surprised when life became more pleasant than it had been before.

I began tailoring Su-Shi's diet to include the nutritional supplements for pregnancy and lactation (see Appendix A) as soon as I got her home. For a nursing mother, calcium and vitamins A, D, and E are especially important. Despite her will-o'-the-wisp appearance, Su-Shi was an enthusiastic gourmand, so I had no problem at all getting the required supplements into her. She would supervise meal preparations from atop the refrigerator, then swoop gleefully down to settle at the plate, sweeping her tail gracefully around herself like the long train of a formal dinner gown before digging in. She purred with enthusiasm all the way through the meal. I fancied it a sort of pussycat *"mes compliments au chef!"* and watched her chow down with immense gratification.

During her sixth week I began giving her a small third meal before bed, watching closely to be sure she didn't gain too much weight. Overweight cats frequently have large kittens and a difficult delivery. I wished fervently that there was some way I could be sure her kittens would not get too big before they were born.

As her pregnancy progressed, my dainty artistocrat began more and more to resemble a small dirigible on stilts. As her abdomen ballooned bigger and bigger, Su-Shi waxed ever more complacent. At night, when she settled herself on my pillow, her soft, soft side pressing against my ear, I began to be aware of subtle stirrings within her—tiny little nudges and thrusts that I could easily feel against my cheek. Su-Shi would sigh and snuggle deeper into the hollow of my neck. It was all "old hat" to her.

During the eighth week her breasts began to swell until her nipples were within an inch of the floor. There was no doubt about it, she was enormous. On the first day of the ninth and final week, I couldn't stand the suspense any longer. I made an appointment with Dr. Van Kluff. I had to be sure her condition was normal.

"Vell, vell, she is about ready, eh?" Dr. Van Kluff beamed. His head was cocked to one side as he listened through the stethoscope to the stirrings inside Su-Shi's belly. As usual Su-Shi's eyes were half-closed with contentment. She lay sprawled on her side and was washing the doctor's wrist.

"What do you think?" I asked. "It will be very soon, won't it? I mean, she certainly can't get any bigger, can she?" My palms were sweating.

Dr. Van Kluff smiled patiently and scratched Su-Shi's head.

"No, no, I think it vill be soon." He looked up. "Does she still eat?"

"Still eat?" I exploded. What was the man talking about! "She's demanding four meals a day now! She's eating like a horse."

Dr. Van Kluff nodded and peered over the rims of his glasses to remind me, "Vell, you know, she vill not eat anymore on the day before her babies are coming."

Then I remembered. Inside the mother, each kitten is encased in its own individual sac. As each kitten is born, the mother breaks the sac and then licks it away so that the kitten can breathe. Then she swallows the sac. This membranous sac contains certain elements which, when the mother cat eats them, send a message to her brain to start the milk flowing into her breasts. Nature provides that the mother will not feel hungry for one day before she gives birth, so her stomach will be empty when it receives the birth sacs, and will send a good clear message to the brain to start the milk flow for the kittens.

That evening Su-Shi ate a very hearty dinner—and a late supper as well. Two days later her appetite was undiminished, but she was having a bit of trouble getting to the food dish. The swollen nipples, jutting out from that enormous blimp of an abdomen, were now brushing the floor when she walked. In between meals she slept a lot and her purring had stopped completely. She was clearly uncomfortable. I called Dr. Van Kluff.

"Vell, vell, so she is a little bit late, eh?" The patient smile projected itself over the phone.

No, no," I explained. "According to the dates I was given, she's due today or tomorrow, but she's still eating like a horse. Now her belly is practically dragging on the floor, and since she's always had small litters, well . . . I'm afraid the kittens are getting too big. What if she can't get them out! Isn't there some way we can find out if everything is all right in there?"

There was a silence at the other end.

"Dr. Van Kluff," I fairly shouted, "she's stopped purring!"

"Hmmmm . . . ya . . . vell . . ." The sound of the patient smile was now absent. "You know, I could give her zomzing to in-juce labor, but, vell, ve don't like to do zat. It iss better, you know, much better ve let Mut-

ter Nature take her course, ya? Zat iss better, always."
That charming old-world accent was getting thicker
by the minute, a sure sign we had him worried.

"But, what if Nature doesn't take its course?" I
asked.

"Vell, vell, you vill call me back tomorrow, ya? I
vill be here."

As for me, I was a complete wreck. Su-Shi lay un-
comfortably on the floor, half under the end table,
constantly shifting her position in an effort to find some
way to settle head and legs around that balloon of a
belly. If we did not "in-juce" labor soon, I was convinced she would rupture.

I sat watching my Su-Shi shift her bloated body
this way and that, unable to relax. The doctor was hes-
itant to interfere with nature because of the risks involved, but I just knew her kittens must be enormous
in there. I had that terrible "damned if I do and
damned if I don't" feeling.

I didn't have any previous experience. The doctor
did. Old Dr. Van Kluff must have seen hundreds of
pregnant queens. I decided to trust the doctor. I would
watch and wait for twelve more hours—then I'd call
him again and, between us, we'd just have to decide
what to do.

I knelt down and scratched down Su-Shi's back the
way she liked, cupping her head in my palm. She relaxed a bit and I had a sudden inspiration. I took a soft
dishtowel from the cupboard, folded it into a little pillow, and slid it gently under her head. I was rewarded
with a deep sigh as she wiggled her balloon into a better position and relaxed into a light sleep.

The owner's thoughts and moods are always com-

municated to the cat. Aware of this, I tried to control
my feelings of rising hysteria. Nevertheless, that afternoon she didn't eat her lunch.

She didn't eat her lunch!

Relief flooded through me. I called the doctor to
report that labor was surely imminent. He agreed to
stand by. "I vill not leaf you, as we say, down the creek,
eh? Heh, heh, heh."

Bless the man! I flew out of the apartment and
down the street to the liquor store for a cardboard box—
not too large in case she wanted to push against the
sides during labor. I brought back three cartons of various sizes; she could choose whichever one she liked.
I cut a gateway in the side of the each carton so that
she could come and go whenever she wanted, but I
left a three-inch-high barrier at the bottom of the entry
way to keep the kittens from falling out.

I had stockpiled plenty of newspaper for a pad on
the bottom of the box. I did not tear it up into small
pieces, because small pieces of paper stick to the kittens and the mother may swallow them as she cleans
her babies.

At six o'clock I offered Su-Shi her dinner, just to
be sure. She gave me a look as if she couldn't figure
out what I expected her to do with it. So I put it aside
and stroked her head and her back down both sides
of the spine, just the way she liked it. Su-Shi readjusted
her dirigible several times and finally went back to
sleep.

At one-thirty in the morning, just as I was getting
into bed, I heard her stirring around in the living room.
I nipped down the hall, turned on the table light, and
sure enough, Su-Shi had chosen one of the boxes. She

was sprawled over on one hip, her front legs propped stiffly up in front of her. She had what looked like a wet mouse dangling from a string in her mouth. Good grief! I realized it was a kitten, a tiny little pink and white mousey-looking kitten. Su-Shi was chewing and chewing the afterbirth, which was attached to the kitten's umbilical cord and, as she chewed, the dangling kitten was being drawn inexorably closer to Su-Shi's grinding teeth. Then, just as the kitten reached her mouth, she gave a neat little nip, bit cleanly through the cord, and the kitten went plunk onto the paper in the bottom of the box. She nudged it over into a corner, then turned away, apparently content to let it lie there all alone.

I leaned closer to examine the kitten, stroking Su-Shi's head and back all the while. It had pink skin, sparse white fur, a pudgy little face, and almost no visible ears. The little pink feet were actually translucent. Siamese kittens are all white at birth; the darker fur on the ears, feet, nose, and tail develops slowly over the first two to four weeks. A baby anything usually looks wrinkled and scrawny until it gets in a few good nursing sessions and starts to put on flesh. Newborn Siamese kittens look as if they shouldn't even have been born yet.

All of those books I'd been reading had been explicit about not overhandling newborn kittens. I do have a tendency to be overcautious, so I was thoroughly programmed. I would practically cut off my hand before I'd even *think* of violating a kitten's sacred person with so much as a fingertip. The reasons for this rule were at first not clear to me. I had assumed that it was because of the kitten's extreme delicacy—

until I saw that umbilical cord procedure with the kitten dangling and jerking in mid-air and dropping with a thud onto the paper. Then I remembered the dark rumors I had heard about mother cats eating their own kittens if someone else touches them. Now, years later, I know that although this *can* happen, it is an extremely rare occurrence. Usually it is caused by some terrible and sudden danger, either real or imagined. When this happens, the mother cat frantically begins picking up the babies in her mouth to carry them to safety. Sometimes, in her distress and confusion, she will begin swallowing the babies because she is trying to pick them all up at once and she has nowhere else to put them except back inside herself where she knows they'll be safe.

I can understand how a new owner, seeing for the first time a cat cleaning a newborn kitten and swallowing the placenta, might confuse this perfectly normal behavior with the other abnormal terror reaction.

Su-Shi was stretched out on her side again, bracing her back feet against the side of the box. She began to push and stretch and purr louder than I had ever heard before. She stretched and pressed with her feet and, as her purr began to crescendo, out slid one more wet little squirmy kitten in a shiny sac. Instantly Su-Shi got to work and, with her prickly tongue, began to lick and lick that membrane away from the little kitten's nose. She kept right on licking and swallowing until there she was again, with the umbilical cord between her teeth and the kitten dangling at the end of it. She gave a neat little nip and one more kitten went plop onto the paper in the bottom of the box. And that was the end of that. I had never seen any creature so relaxed and in command of a situation as was my efficient little Su-Shi, seeing to the business of ushering her kittens into the world. Her purr vibrated through the living room and a swooping crescendo like a sort of pussycat fanfare accompanied the entrance of each new little soul into the world.

Su-Shi was a prima donna, the star of the show in her greatest role, and she was insistent that I witness the entire performance. Only once I tried leaving the room, but I returned double-quick when Su-Shi came leaping out of the box and called me back with loud and indignant cries. So I settled myself down on the floor by the box and watched her produce the very grand total of six squirmy little pink and white kittens. Good grief! No wonder she had blown up like a blimp! An unpredictable Mother Nature was laughing at my hopes for a small litter.

My little princess was a natural mother; she threw a litter as easily as rolling off a log. I was among the luckiest of owners.

It doesn't always happen that way. Persian cats especially are now being bred to have very large heads and tiny hips, a shape so against Nature that the necessity for a ceasarean section is becoming more and more frequent, and death due to difficult labor a not uncommon occurrence. For any cat it is always wise to have a veterinarian whom you can contact if the birth doesn't seem to be going well.

It is perfectly normal for kittens to emerge head first or tail first—either way is fine. However, prolonged pushing without results, crying out during labor, or having a kitten stop when only halfway through the birth canal are signs of serious trouble. The owner should be prepared to scoop up box, mother, and kittens and rush them to the veterinarian.

If you are ever in a situation where a kitten is stuck halfway and no help is available, first stroke the mother's back and encourage her to push against your hand. If this fails, you may grasp the kitten and *slowly*, very, very slowly, urge and pull the kitten out, preferably in rhythm with the mother's pushing.

Another caution: Be very sure that every kitten and all of the afterbirths have been expelled. Postnatal piometria (uterine infection) due to unexpelled afterbirth is a heartbreakingly frequent cause of feline death. If the mother seems at all tired or lethargic during the first week after the kittens are born, don't wait. Get her to the veterinarian and have her checked out.

Su-Shi's kittens had all arrived safely in two-and-a-half hours. It was four A.M. Su-Shi was tired; I was exhausted. But the grand finale was just about to begin.

This was the scene to which Su-Shi had been building for nine long weeks. She stood up, circled once around the box and lay down again, this time on her side with her swollen breasts pressed up against the pile of kittens in the corner. That comatose heap of kittens reacted as if Su-Shi had sent an electric current through them. They fairly exploded into six lively, flailing little bundles of appetite. They opened their tiny mouths and gave forth little chirpy sounds of "weee . . . weee . . . pweee!" like six baby birds when the mother lands on the nest. They scrabbled with their weak little feet against the floor and against each other, trying to gain a nipple. Su-Shi calmly nudged and licked first one then another into line, until all six were nuzzling at a breast. But it looked like no one had yet figured out just how to get the nipple into his mouth. Six little noses were searching vigorously up and down, and around and back and forth and every which way around the nipples which, in turn, were bounding and springing all about the little noses but never inside the little mouths. I was feeling mighty anxious about this time, but Su-Shi was still purring away, obviously in complete control of the situation. The kittens were still crying their tiny obbligato, "pweee. . . pwee! pweee!" Then, suddenly, once again, Su-Shi's purr began to crescendo to a roar—obviously an orchestral cue of some sort. She stretched and arched her whole body out, then curled herself in around her squirming family and began to lick each of the little heads three or four times. As she licked, her rough tongue pushed each kitten out and away from the nipple. The kitten reacted by "pweee-ing" and pushing even more strongly with its little legs. After three or four licks, Su-Shi would stop abruptly and the force of the kitten's struggle against her would carry it bang into the swollen breast. The impact must have released some scent of milk because each kitten got the nipple right into its mouth without any trouble at all after that.

This routine was repeated six times until all the "pweeing" was silent. The little mouths pulled and sucked and the tiny paws with tiny, almost hair-like nails, pushed and kneaded at Su-Shi's breasts. As her brood drained the milk and relieved her breasts, her purr became a veritable symphony with overtones and bass notes that filled the cardboard box and the whole living room with warm and sonorous joy.

Before I dropped into bed, I rigged a 75-watt light over the box to be sure mother and babies would be warm. The Siamese is a tropical cat. I decided a light snack was in order, and Su-Shi came trotting out of the box to eat with great relish a small dish of food liberally laced with the vitamins for nursing mothers and a half-cup of High Calcium Chicken Broth (see Appendix A).

The newspaper in the bottom of the box was a mess of blood, water, and sticky pieces of placenta, so, while Su-Shi was eating, I lifted the whole thing out, kittens and all, put in a clean new pad of newspapers, then carefully slid the sleeping kittens back onto that. During all this, the little mother, blissfully unconcerned, never missed a lap of her food.

After she snuggled back down in her nice clean box with her nice new kittens, I stroked her down the back again the way she always liked it and told her what a magnificent and wondrous creature she was. Then, with great daring and the utmost care and caution, I touched and stroked the tip of my finger over every single little kitten. Su-Shi squinted contentedly, and as she drifted off to sleep, her soft purr seemed to sing, "Sleep in peace, my kittens, for life is good, and the world is a fine place!" I realized with a sigh of resignation that it was up to me to find six owners who would see to it that it stayed that way.

Piccola's Story

JAMES FRANCIS VAX   CRIS ARBO

CHAPTER TWO

SPICCOLA'S
TORY:

Kittens—The First Eight Weeks

As SOON as her kittens are born and start nursing, the mother cat's appetite changes from voracious to insatiable. She should be given four large, nutritious meals a day. As the kittens grow, they require more and more milk. The mother's needs increase proportionately, and when her babies are about five weeks old, she will eat up to six meals a day without gaining weight.

If the mother cannot get enough of the right foods to manufacture milk for the kittens, then her own body must supply the missing nutrients. Her body will consume itself, converting fat and muscle tissue into food for the hungry litter. Calcium will be drawn from her bones, which will then become porous and brittle. Her coat will become dull and shed copiously.

Sad examples of such pitifully depleted females can be seen running wild on the streets of any city. The one I got to know lived in New York City's Little Italy, in an alley behind Di Pietro's Italian restaurant.

The drama of La Piccola Mamma opened with an urgent phone call.

The familiar gravel voice and Italian accent at the other end came from Louie Di Pietro (pronounced dee PEE tro). He and his wife, Angela, ran a small gourmet restaurant in the heart of Little Italy on New York's Lower East Side. Their black and white short-hair, Spats, had been a client of mine for years.

Louie was excited. "Madonna mia, five a' them, Anitra, in a old wood crate. And that mamma cat, I'm tellin ya, she looks thin, like a bone!"

Dear Louie, big and strong and loud, with a heart like a giant marshmallow; he knew enough about cats to know that a skinny little mother with five kittens to nurse represented an emergency situation. But before I could help, I needed a few facts. "How old do the kittens look to you, Louie?"

"What do I know!" Louie's voice took on a note of helpless panic. "Maybe dey're just born or somethin'. Angela just put 'em in a big salad bowl, and we took 'em all home.

"That mamma, she's wild, Anitra, she won't let nobody near 'er. But when we took the babies, she just come runnin' along behind. So now we got the whole family down under the stairs in the storeroom."

I knew the storeroom. It was clean and dry. The stairs to it led off the kitchen. You could look down and see neatly stacked crates of olive oil and tomato paste.

Looking out my office window, I could see large wet snowflakes falling past and disappearing into the alley below. It was as cold and wet and windy as a day in February can be. I wondered how long the little cat had been making it on her own in the back alleys. That little female was lucky to get herself "captured" when she did.

Louie went on, his voice lowered to a confidential tone. "Listen, Anitra, we have got ourselves a *sitcheeashun* here, 'cause those kittens, they are all fulla fleas. Angela, she says we gotta clean 'em up quick or else we are gonna have fleas all over the storeroom, ya know?

"And that ain't all, Anitra." I braced myself, wondering what more the "sitcheeashun" needed to make it complete. "That mamma cat, she don't look so good to me, 'cause a couple a minutes ago she started gettin' all stiff and shaky and she was kinda chewin' at the air with her mouth open. You ever hear of somethin' like that before?"

Unfortunately I had. It sounded like a case of eclampsia, sometimes called calcium fits. A nursing female can have convulsions brought on by a lack of calcium in her diet. This little cat had been on her way to a better world when Louie and Angela Di Pietro happened along.

"It's because she's starving, Louie," I began.

"Oh, don't worry, Anitra, we give her a good meal right away—a nice big plate of pasta. Madonna mia, she could eat!"

I'll bet she did, I thought. But there's precious little calcium in pasta.

"She needs calcium, Louie—and fast. Some fats and oils would go down nicely too. I'll tell you what you can do. Have Angela give her a saucer of half-and-half, or maybe a little ricotta, and mix in a half-teaspoon of that cod liver oil you keep for Spats." I was taking a chance. Many adult cats get diarrhea from milk products, which, in this cat's weakened condition could be fatal, but I really didn't have much choice. I had to work fast and I had to use what the Di Pietros were likely to have on hand. I'd have felt better if she could have had a calcium shot, but even if Louie could catch her and then get her into a carry case, I knew there were no vets' offices near the restaurant, and it was past office hours anyway. Hopefully her body would absorb the calcium in the milk quickly enough with the help of the vitamin D in the cod liver oil.

"I'll stop by later this evening, Louie, after I finish the evening feeding and medications for the cats up here."

Louie was a man reprieved. "You'll stay to supper, Anitra. Let me tell Angie you'll stay. We got manicotti from my mother tonight." I accepted with pleasure. Mamma Di Pietro's manicotti was a house specialty that drew repeat customers from as far away as Palermo.

I lucked out on the subways and made the trip downtown in thirty-five minutes. Angela in her starchy apron was waiting to let me in the back way. She ushered me down to the storeroom where La Piccola Mamma, the little mother, as she called her, was nicely settled in with her kittens.

They were nestled together in a wine crate under the stairs. It was turned on its side with one of the restaurant's red and white checkered tablecloths folded neatly in the bottom. And there, lying curled around her brood, was a cobby little gray and white short-hair with very Persian bone structure. I know the type well; extremely healthy and resilient. If any cat could survive on the street, she could. But the cat lying in that box had clearly reached the end of her rope. Pitifully thin and dirty, she couldn't have been more than eight or nine months old herself. Her belly was puffed out like a balloon, evidence that the Di Pietro's generosity had been a bit overdone. Apparently the poor cat had eaten until she could hardly breathe. The rest of her was skin and bone—ribs ridging the chest, front legs like sticks, and a head that swayed weakly on a neck too skinny to support its weight. She lowered her chin and regarded us with big watchful eyes.

The kittens lay against their mother, an amorphous pile of noses, tails and paws, sleeping the sleep of the innocent. I became aware of small movements and realized I was witnessing the leisurely progress of several large brown fleas across tiny thighs and abdomens. Piccola began washing a little gray head, her tongue passing expertly between the ears, down the shoulders, down the back, and out the tail. Fleas often carry tapeworm. I made a mental note to have the whole group tested once we got rid of the fleas. It would be easy enough to do—we would simply send a fresh stool sample from each cat to the veterinarian to be examined under the microscope. But first I had to get rid of the fleas. That meant I would have to handle and bathe all the cats. How would Piccola Mamma feel about that?

I would have to proceed very slowly, so I figured I'd better start introducing myself right away. Cats are very polite. I would have to use maximum tact and pay strict attention to feline etiquette. Moving closer to the wine carton, I seated myself casually on the floor, facing slightly away from Piccola Mamma. By being seated and facing away, I was not as threatening. Casually I let my hand come to rest palm down on the floor about six inches from her nose. I still did not intrude with eye contact, but let her get a good sniff of me "behind my back," as it were.

Just then the door above flew open and Louie's big frame appeared and started down the stairs, white apron flapping.

"Anitra, Angie didn't feed ya!" he shouted over the clump of his own heavy shoes. "I told Angie she should feed ya first!"

Angela replied with a gentle ripple of Italian. She spoke English well enough but preferred to use Italian when she spoke to Louie. They had been childhood sweethearts, growing up together "in the neighborhood," as Louie put it. Louie adored his quiet wife with a profound and protective love, which he attempted to conceal from the world behind a facade of bluster and gruffness. Angela, for her part, responded with the gentle tolerance of a madonna. They were one of my favorite couples.

During this distraction I made a point to slowly turn and, for a brief second, look directly at Piccola Mamma. I caught her eye, blinked once, then let my attention wander casually back to Louie. In other words, I gently added eye contact and acknowledged that we were aware of each other's presence. I repeated this contact several times while we continued talking.

"Louie," I interrupted, "I don't want to alarm you

and Angela, but we do have something of an emergency here."

I had their immediate attention.

"If we don't want the Piccola Mamma to have a convulsion again, we've got to build that body of hers up before it stops functioning altogether."

I went on to explain that a nursing mother needs frequent small, high-quality meals with plenty of protein, calcium, and fats. Feeding a large meal, as Angela did, is not a good idea, because a cat like that is too weak to digest so much at once. If you overcrowd her stomach, she'll either vomit or pass the food through without getting the good of it. Even her digestive juices will be weak, so it is more efficient to give her only about a half-cup of food at a time. However, she should be fed every three hours or so for a day or two, then hopefully she will be well enough to handle four to five medium-sized meals a day. Quality is the watchword; quantity can actually work against you.

The Di Pietros were nodding vigorously. I gave Angela the recipe for my High Calcium Chicken Broth (see Appendix A), a good source of calcium and protein, and she went flying up the steps, the consummate chef armed with her trusty soup ladle, setting out to battle the ravages of starvation.

Turning my attention back to Piccola Mamma, I decided now that she had accepted my smell and had returned my eye contact, it was time to add voice and then touch.

When talking to a nervous cat, you must carefully choose your words. She may not understand language, but she will pick up your emotional attitude. Since words communicate the emotional attitude you want to broadcast, you can strengthen your communication simply by saying in words what you feel inside. Caution: *Do not lie.* Cats recognize duplicity. If you lie, the cat will sense your insincerity and will not trust you.

So now all I had to do was convey to a filthy, suspicious, flea-ridden cat my honest admiration and reassurance. I looked at her there, curled protectively around those tiny kittens and suddenly it was easy.

First I reestablished eye contact. "Piccola, oh Piccola," I said and blinked. Eye contact must not be too sustained or it can become threatening, so I had to remember to blink now and then all during the conversation.

"What a large family you have, Piccola, and they're such good little kittens." Blink. Piccola blinked back. I was making progress.

We were both beaming at her kittens. I guessed that they were about a week and a half old, but it was hard to tell exactly. They had an unnatural, spidery look; their bodies were too long and thin, their heads looked too big for the rest of them. Piccola Mamma's starving body had not been able to provide enough milk for them.

"Piccola," I caught her eye again, "we're going to give you delicious food to make your body strong again." Blink. She blinked and lowered her head to her paws, watching me.

I could just imagine what her life must have been like, a typical surplus cat, thrown onto the street.

Many a young, healthy female has made it on her own by hunting mice and eating garbage. She'll find a dry spot to sleep, in a deserted cellar or under a pile of junk in an alley. She'll get along just fine. That is, until she comes into her first heat.

Veterinarians will tell you a cat should not be bred during her first heat. That would be like letting a twelve-year-old girl have a baby; it's possible, but definitely not a good idea. Piccola Mamma must have come into season when she was about six or seven months old and attracted a wild Tom who impregnated her.

Females who have litters in the warm weather are lucky. They are more likely to survive, especially if their litter is small or if part of the litter is destroyed by dogs or wandering Toms. A small litter is not so big a drain on the mother's body, and if the weather is warm, calories are not burned just to maintain body temperature.

But Piccola had her kittens early in February. Old snow still lay on the ground; it thawed to slush during the day and froze again at night. Hunting is next to impossible in ice and snow, and garbage cans are often frozen shut. I couldn't help wondering how she managed to survive, this game little mother.

I noticed her tiny hip bones, two protruding bumps in her lower back, which shouldn't be visible. Normally they are hidden under fat and muscle. I could picture her wading up to her ankles through the slush, clutching in her jaws some half-eaten piece of garbage. I'd be willing to bet that little body hadn't known stored fat since before the kittens were born.

"Piccola." I called her attention to my hand, moving and lifting it. Then I extended a finger toward her chin, stopped, and let her sniff it. She didn't move away, so

I continued slowly moving the finger to touch her head, then stroke behind the ears and down the neck, talking all the while. "Piccola is the bravest and the best little mother in all the world. *E vero*, Louie? Isn't that true?"

I gave a last blink and turned to Louie, who was staring at us, spellbound. I wanted to let Piccola rest for a while, undisturbed, so I stood up.

"And now, Louie," I said as I brushed off my jeans, "I believe you mentioned something about manicotti."

Louie, beaming, led the way, clumping up the stairs.

There is nothing the Di Pietros love more than to see someone enjoying their food. And there is no food I love more than Mamma Di Pietro's manicotti. The outside is a light, spongy little Italian *crêpe* that sops up and holds the tomato sauce. And the ricotta inside is like a compressed cloud, puffing out at both ends. The mozzarella lies there glimmering on top like a golden pool of contentment, and then trails glistening threads of delight behind as you waft the forkful to your lips. I ate five, as usual, with Spats cheering me on and Louie chiding me for leaving the sixth un-touched—as usual.

Now I was nicely fueled for the main event.

I avoid using chemical flea preparations whenever possible. If an owner insists upon it, I use only the preparations in which pyrethrins are the active ingre-dients and only the ones specifically for cats that I get from the veterinarian. I use it exactly as directed, with the precisely correct time span between applications, and I dose the animal with antitoxin supplements for a week before and a month after the treatment. Even with all these precautions, I don't advise the use of chemicals. A cat's skin easily absorbs anything you put on it. To use a chemical preparation on two-week-old kittens and a nursing mother in weakened condition would be like signing their death warrant. Thorough bathing was the only answer.

Fleas drown easily. When you bathe an animal, the fleas run up to its head, heading for the high ground. So you can simply comb them out of the head, cheeks, and jowls, and plunk them into a waiting bowl of water.

Many people have a mental block against bathing a cat. I love it because it's a sure way to make the cat feel absolutely wonderful.

So, Louie and I made plans for making five very skinny two-week-old kittens and one very wild and terrified mother feel absolutely wonderful—and incidentally getting rid of the fleas.

I had decided to bathe Piccola first to demonstrate to her exactly what I intended to do. Then I hoped she wouldn't become hysterical when I started in on her kittens. I managed to murmur and blink my way into a lounging position right next to Piccola's box, hoping she would permit me to take up where we left off earlier. She consented to sniff my finger and then, tilting her head, she stretched forward and pressed one ear into the palm of my hand. I was overwhelmed! She was asking me to stroke her, and I knew in that moment when I felt her ear brush my palm that Piccola had loved very dearly the human who put her out on the street.

"Pearls before swine, little lady," I told her. "Don't you worry, my Piccola; you, my dear, have fallen into a pot of jam."

Her hair felt like dry bristles. As I lightly stroked

her muzzle, I could have sworn I felt her fang wiggle. Well, I wasn't surprised. It was just another sign of malnutrition; probably all her teeth were loose.

I had Louie lay out everything I would need. He attached my rubber hose to the spigot, adjusted the water temperature, and left it running to warm the tub.

The kittens would have to be kept warm while the mother was being bathed, and we needed a new box for the clean family members, so while Piccola and I continued to get to know each other I sent Louie to collect three empty plastic bottles and three heavy socks. I asked him to fill the bottles with very hot water and drop each into a sock; then I placed them among the sleeping kittens. Now they would stay warm and snug while their mamma was away having her bath.

Piccola had almost certainly never had a bath before; I wanted to make her first experience as pleasant as possible.

She came into my arms readily enough when invited, the top of her head nestled beneath my chin. I rocked her and pleaded, "Oh please don't think I'm a traitor, little lady, when I put you into that wet tub."

Piccola cried out when I lowered her into the tub. It was the first time I had heard her voice and it was so filled with despair, I wished we could just forget the whole thing; but, of course, we couldn't. So I nestled my face close to hers and pointed out how nice and warm the tub was. Keeping your face close reassures a cat that the situation is safe. A cat knows that the face and eyes are vulnerable; there is a basic instinct to protect them. Therefore, when you first meet a cat, it is a very friendly gesture to extend your nose because you are demonstrating trust by exposing your

vulnerable parts. In the same way, by voluntarily placing my face and eyes close to Piccola Mamma's while
broadcasting calm and loving emotions and words, I
was, in effect, telling her that this activity was harmless—maybe a bit odd, but definitely not dangerous.

The human mind is, in many ways, more powerful
than a pussycat mind; and if you use honesty as a tool,
you can greatly influence a cat's emotions. I don't mean
that you actually change them; but, by choosing what
elements to focus your mind on in any given situation,
you can gently redirect a cat's thoughts and emotions
and rechannel them along more peaceful, pleasurable,
or reassuring lines.

Never ask a cat to stand in water—the feeling is far
too alien. The cat should stand in an empty but warm
tub. I introduced the warm water from the hose only
on her outer thigh at first, holding the hose so the water
came out in my palm. I saturated her coat with water,
keeping my hand with the hose close to her body at
all times so that all she felt was a gentle stroking of
warmth. I left her face dry because she was perfectly
capable of washing it herself. After the coat was thoroughly wet, I applied the warm, fragrant shampoo and
water mixture, working from the neck down, lathering
the body, and nuzzling and murmuring compliments
as I combed huge fleas from the head, cheeks, and chin
and plunked them into Louie's waiting bowl of water.
The whole time I kept my face close to hers and kept
the tip of the hose resting in my palm. One should
never let a cat see water flying at her. I had adjusted
the water temperature to a delicious warmth, so I
called her attention to that. As I soaped her up, I
pointed out how good it smelled and recalled to her

how nice it was to be clean and free of fleas. I told her that her colors would be beautiful again, that her skin would stop itching, and, as I massaged the soap down her gaunt little chest and legs, I told her how Louie and Angela loved her and would make her strong and happy again.

And Piccola believed me. She stood there tense and trembling and barely able to control her surging emotions, but she did believe me because it was all true and because *I* believed me. She believed everything I said; but she also believed that I was one of the most peculiar human beings she had ever run across.

And that was all right too, because there was no despair and no terror in that. If she had any complaints, she was entitled to her opinion.

She cried out again when I soaped her up the third time. She felt, quite reasonably, that enough was enough and it was time to get back to her kittens. But even one flea egg lodging in the hair follicles will eventually hatch, and if it finds a mate, they can start a whole new infestation. It would have been foolhardy to skimp on the bath once she was wet.

Never ignore a cat when she complains during a procedure. If you want her to feel safe and allow you to finish, you must acknowledge her complaints and let her know you understand and are working toward fulfilling her wishes.

I wasn't able to get her to really enjoy the bath— that was too much to expect. But I did manage to turn terror and fear into the much more manageable feeling of exasperation at the stupidity of this peculiar human.

Then, when the bath was all over and Piccola Mamma was dry, well . . . she was a smart cat. Preening and stretching her clean dry body, she put two and two together and knew at last what the bath was all about. She would, of course, have preferred it if I had used my tongue, as any sensible cat would do, but humans, she had already decided, were a peculiar lot who had their own peculiar way of doing things, and being clean again was, after all, a lovely feeling.

One at a time we bathed the kittens in a mixing bowl. Angela took away their old crate which was full of flea eggs and debris while Louie held the little ones in his lap. I lowered them one by one up to the neck in warm soapy water until their back toes touched the bottom and the bubbles were tickling their chins. Kittens this young have to be immersed when they're bathed in order to keep them warm. I combed the fleas out of the kittens' heads and dropped them into the waiting cup of water to drown. The kittens were then rinsed in two other bowls of clear water and dried surprisingly quickly with paper towels and the blow dryer. There is absolutely nothing quite so efficient as paper towels for drying a kitten.

Piccola paced and called and worried until she had the first little fellow safely back with her. Then she licked him, examining him all over with her tongue to be sure I had done him no harm, and by the time she was through, we had the next one ready for her approval; and so we finished the whole litter with no further complaint from her.

When the cleanup was finished and my equipment put away, we found ourselves standing by Piccola's box admiring the little family. Now that everyone was clean, we could finally see what they looked like. None of them had much hair. Pink skin showed through the pitifully sparse little coats.

There were two whites with gray spots. They were

the skinniest; they looked as if the father had a little Siamese blood. Then there were two all-whites who were heavier boned like their cobby mother, and a tortoise-shell who stood out from the others because she was so dark. Piccola must have been fertilized on two occasions by two separate males, one very lanky and one more cobby, like a Persian. Since females only release one egg each time they are fertilized, it is possible, though not usual, for a litter to have as many fathers as there are kittens.

The kittens began to stir, nuzzling for the nipples. Swimming does make one hungry. One by one they nosed their way in to Piccola's soft breasts and began to nurse—all except one. I should have expected it. We had a runt, a skinny little gray and white problem who lay helplessly at the side of the box giving occasional soft little cries of "pweee-pweee." Piccola gave him two or three gentle licks with her tongue and then turned away, giving all her attention to the nursing group.

To a mother cat there is no such thing as equal and fair distribution of milk. From her point of view, if kittens are nursing and breasts are being drained, all is as it should be. Mother cats don't know how to count noses. For this reason it is wise for the owner to supervise nursing at least three or four times a day. This is done during the first three weeks to be sure that a runt is not created because one kitten is repeatedly being pushed away. In the wild, a runt will simply die of starvation. This serves the valuable function of weeding out the weaklings and leaving more milk for the strong who are better able to survive anyway. And, because there is less drain on the mother, she too will have a better chance for survival.

Louie lifted the little gray and white kitten over to Piccola and made a place for her among the others. After the kittens had eaten, I asked Louie for some vegetable food coloring and I put a tiny blue dot in the kitten's armpit for identification purposes. Louie and Angela would then be able to keep track of Sweet Little Alice Blue Dot, as she came to be called, and be sure she made it to a nipple at least four times a day.

Angela had the pleasurable task of building up the health of the little family with the delicious food she fed them. The first night, for a bedtime snack, Piccola Mamma had a dish of Spats's food, which Angela always made from my recipe (see Basic Diet III, Appendix A). The next day Angela got the Pregnancy and Lactation Supplements (Appendix A) from the health food store and added them to the food as well. This, plus the High Calcium Chicken Broth (Appendix A) I knew would do the trick in no time. Kittens respond very quickly to dietary improvement, and Piccola Mamma was little more than a kitten herself, so I expected to see results within a week or two. As it turned out I was not disappointed.

Dinner the next Thursday at the Di Pietros was something of a celebration. Piccola Mamma and her family were definitely out of the woods.

This time I came in the front entrance of the restaurant in order to greet Spats. I felt guilty about not giving him any attention on my last visit, but I had had my hands full with Piccola Mamma. Tonight he would have his usual grooming and pedicure.

Spats was posed beside the cash register on the front counter, available for greetings, pettings, and giving friendly welcomes to customers old and new. Dressed formally, as always: white ruff, white spats, black suit and tail—Spats gave a tone of old-world elegance to the place. Spats had been on his way to the ASPCA to be "disposed of" when Louie spotted him. "Leave 'im with me," he had said to the owner, "I like his face." Spats repaid Louie's generosity by simultaneously creating and filling the function of *maitre d'*.

"Look at this bum, Anitra."

Louie began stroking the cat's head, neck and back with practiced hands and Spats sprawled out on the glass countertop the better to enjoy the massage.

"He lies around all day, he don't do no work, an' then he eats me out a' house an' home." Spats rolled over to present his other side for Louie's petting. "One a' these days, out he goes. Ya hear that, ya bum? No more free meal ticket if ya don't shape up." Spats was trying to knead the counter with his paws.

Louie positively doted on the cat so, as was his habit, he tried to cover his affection with the usual gruff bluster. Spats obviously took it for what it was: a mark of Louie's deep affection.

When Spats' grooming and pedicure were finished, I insisted on seeing Piccola Mamma and the kittens before sitting down to dinner.

What a change one week of good food and safety can make! The kittens were snuggled happily in the wine box, asleep against Piccola's soft breasts. They looked fluffy! And they were beginning to fill out a bit too. They looked almost like normal kittens now. Piccola stood up, daintily disengaging herself from her sleeping babies. She stretched and yawned, relaxed and at home now, digging her claws into the floor of the box. She was beautiful. Now that her nutritional needs were being met, she was regaining her natural strength and grace.

I reintroduced myself and felt with pleasure the new softness of her fur and a hint of flesh around her protruding hip bones. I stroked down her back, hard, and was delighted to hear her purr and feel her pushing up against my hand. Her muscle tone was returning very nicely indeed.

"They look beautiful, Louie. You and Angela have done a terrific job."

Louie beamed. "It was Angie mostly. They look good, huh?"

I stood up. "I wouldn't be surprised if she starts litter box training her kittens next week."

"Hey, that's great!" Louie started clumping up the stairs. "Angie'll be glad to hear that. She was wondering, ya know?"

The following Monday night, Louie's voice was among the others on my answering machine. "Anitra, this is Louie Di Pietro. We got ourselves a sitcheea-shun here. These kittens, they're goin' to the bathroom all over the cellar. I don't know what Piccola's doin.' Ya know? She ain't gettin 'em all into the litter in time or somethin'. Could you give us a call, please?"

I sat a while at my desk and thought about the problem before I called Louie back. I had to move fast. Nature has provided certain time periods in a kitten's life when imprinting will easily occur and the kitten will learn almost automatically that which it is supposed to be learning at that particular time. The time for toilet training was going on right now, and it sounded as if Piccola needed some help before the time ran out.

I quickly fed and medicated the group at my place, then poured myself a glass of cider and settled at the desk to return my phone messages. I made the Di Pietros first on the list.

Louie sounded a little discouraged as he explained his sitcheeashun. "Listen, Anitra, what's happenin' is, Piccola ain't doin' such a good job, ya know? Angela, she keeps finding pieces of baby kitten dirt all over the place and she's all upset because she's afraid somebody's gonna send a health inspector and he's gonna make us get rid of the kittens."

"Don't worry, Louie," I said, "I've seen this problem before. In fact, I went through the same thing myself a few years ago. But in a day or two I got the situation under control. Tell Angie not to worry. If you like, I'll drop by later tonight."

"Great, Anitra, just great!" Louie was his old hearty self again. "You'll stay to dinner, okay? Let me tell Angie you'll stay."

As usual, I accepted with pleasure.

Louie and Angela did not insist that I eat dinner before seeing the cats that night. Instead, the three of us filed down the old wooden steps to see what we could do about the Di Pietros' latest problem.

The kittens had been playing with a two-foot length of clothesline. It lay discarded at the foot of the steps and there, near the far end, was a tiny stool. Piccola's litter box lessons were definitely not paying off. And when I looked at the family group together in the wine crate, I got a pretty good idea why.

Angela must have been in her glory for the past week and a half. After devouring meal after meal of delicious, nourishing food, Piccola Mamma had finally been able to provide an abundance of milk for her babies. Well, those spindly little kittens were spindly no more. Proud Piccola, modestly licking the nearest pink ear, was still a very small cat, sleek and contented, but small. But her kittens, I swear, had nearly doubled in size.

"They're beautiful, Louie," I exclaimed and knelt down by the box. Piccola ceased her washing of the kitten's ear and gave me a welcoming blink.

"Yeah," Louie beamed, "they're all gettin' fat; that's Angela's doin'.""

Angela laughed softly, "She was so hungry, La Piccola Mamma," and she knelt on the floor beside me, whereupon Piccola gently disengaged herself from her fuzzy progeny and jumped lightly onto Angela's lap.

Louie got right down to brass tacks. "Listen, Anitra, you got any idea of what we're gonna do about this sitcheeashun we got here?"

Happily I did. The situation looked to me to be just about the same as when I'd had the problem years ago: The litter box had too much litter in it and the kittens were getting too big for the mother to lift easily.

Cleaning away body wastes is a very basic instinct in any cat. Adult cats in the wild go far away from the nest to bury their wastes. The reason is simple: body wastes have a strong smell and a strong smell can attract predators. Obviously when the nest is full of tiny kittens, it's even more important to be sure no odor will give away the location. Since the tiny babies aren't able to leave the nest themselves to pass wastes, nature provides an alternative. The mother cat licks the kitten's abdominal and anal area to stimulate the response of passing urine and stool; she then swallows the wastes before they can soil the nest. These wastes pass through her body to be disposed of later with her own body wastes. This instinct for cleanliness is strong because it has to do directly with the preservation of life. It is ingrained deeply into a cat's subconscious and is a basic part of feline nature.

As toilet training time approaches, it is wise to keep the litter box scrupulously clean and not to put too much litter in. I should have warned the Di Pietros about too much litter. An eighth of an inch is quite enough, otherwise tiny legs will sink in up to the hip.

At that moment, as if on cue, Piccola wriggled out of Angela's arms and went padding over to the litter box, trilling her soft kitten call as she hopped into the box and stood waiting. The kittens paid no attention whatsoever. At three-and-a-half weeks no one expected them to, least of all Piccola Mamma. But she knew that there would come a time when they would remember what it is that always comes after their mother's call from the litter box, and then they would come running to the box on their own. But in the meantime, Piccola had the patience that comes with love.

She trotted over to her family, picked up the nearest kitten, who happened to be one of the little white chunky ones and, with the kitten's entire head between her jaws and its stubby tail dragging on the floor, struggled over and plunked it into the litter box.

The litter, of course, was much too deep. The kitten took one teetering step and sank in up to his elbows. Two pieces of litter got stuck to his nose and he immediately began to eat it. None too steady under the very best of circumstances, his short little legs kept sinking in thigh deep and he kept tripping and falling and getting more pieces of litter stuck to his nose, which he would lick off and swallow.

Neither the kitten nor his mother were the least bit perturbed by this situation. Heedless of the problem on the front end, Piccola pressed on with the project of training the back end. She came up behind the little fellow, who was swaying precariously as he struggled unsuccessfully to deal with a particularly stubborn flake of litter stuck to the corner of his mouth, and began licking his anal area, to trigger the response of passing wastes. The kitten stopped fighting with the litter flake and an expression of deep and serious concentration appeared on his face. Still swaying unsteadily, he began to squat down, the tiny tail pointing straight out behind. He froze motionless and out came several drops of urine which disappeared into the litter.

"Bravo!" I whispered. Angela smiled and nodded. And Piccola began covering the kitten with warm licks of praise. Of course, this knocked him down again. Head over heels he went, into the litter, all the time responding to the licks with delighted little wiggles and kicks of pleasure while Louie suppressed a gale of laughter, one hand clapped tightly across his mouth. Suddenly Piccola stopped and abruptly trotted off to fetch the second kitten. I reached over for number one, dusted him off and put him back on the floor; then quickly scooped most of the litter into the trash can, leaving only an eighth of an inch on the bottom of the box. The next kitten would find it easier to keep his balance and, hopefully, there would be less falling down and no litter on the nose.

It worked out very nicely. The scene was repeated

twice more but that was all. I hoped that these three were the kittens who had most recently nursed and that Piccola would attend to her other two at a later time.

As if to reassure us, a couple of hours later when we came down again after dinner, Piccola put three little kittens through their paces in the litter box. But again, only three.

Louie assured me, "She's been doin' it like that since yesterday, Anitra, every couple a' hours she takes three a' them in the litter and still we got little kitten dirt on the floor."

"She can't count noses, Louie," I explained. "It's just like when she was nursing and she didn't know that one of her kittens wasn't getting a nipple. Then, too, you've got to realize how small she is and how difficult it must be to lift even one of those big healthy kittens and hoist it into the litter box. She's exhausted by the time she finishes with three. Since she can't differentiate between kittens, there's a very good possibility that two or three kittens are going to the litter box every single time, while the others aren't being trained at all. We'll just have to help her."

Here is what we did. The waste-passing response is triggered with a warm, moist, rough tongue, so we simply needed to provide something that was warm, moist, and rough.

I cut three pieces from an old washcloth and gave one each to Louie and Angie to wrap around their index finger. I filled a mug with warm water, picked up the other little white kitten and set him in the litter. Dunking my terrycloth-clad finger into a cup of warm water, I placed it between the baby's hind legs, up against his abdomen, and gently stroked backwards a few times across the genital area and out the tail. The only sound in the room was the crunching of litter under the tiny white feet as the kitten began to crouch. The familiar look of deep concentration suffused his face and his little tail pointed straight out behind.

"Bravo!" I whispered, as several drops of urine fell onto the litter.

"*Ecco la!*" breathed Angela, and Louie let out a sigh of relief.

"Now you must praise him," I said, scratching the little white head. My pupil responded with little kittenish wiggles of pleasure, and I lifted him out and returned him to the group.

Louie and Angela could hardly wait to try. They each selected a kitten and began applying their own version of warm, moist, and rough to trigger the kitten's waste-passing response. Within ten minutes all five kittens had made a small deposit in the box.

After about a week of this the kittens were big enough to scramble into the litter box by themselves. Their mother would stand in the middle of the litter and trill her special kitten call, and all five would come scampering and hoist themselves into the box. Then the floor all around the box would be showered with bits of clay as five little kittens threw their hearts and souls into the grown-up business of passing and covering wastes.

Once this hurdle was overcome, I decided it was time to broach the subject of the kittens' future. I felt that they should begin now to look for potential owners. "But they are so little," Angela softly pointed out, plainly distressed at the thought of parting with them.

I think the hardest part of having a litter of kittens is letting them go. Angela and Louie were doubly attached to these kittens because they had literally brought them back from death's door. They had given unstintingly of themselves: their time, their money, their loving concern, and they had grown to love this little family and also to love their own role as protectors and providers. I wanted to make it as easy for them as I possibly could.

"Angela," I explained, "I didn't mean we should let them go now. They're much too young. However, we should start planning now because you and Louie would never let one of these kittens go to a home unless you were sure that it was the very best place for the kitten."

They were both nodding soberly and the lines of worry had left Angela's brow. So, I went on to propose a possible strategy.

First, we could test the sincerity of the prospective owner's concern for the kitten's welfare simply by stipulating that the kittens must all remain with the mother until they were eight weeks old. The reason for this is more than just physical needs. During the first eight weeks, training and imprinting by the mother is taking place. Many important behavior patterns are being passed on by the mother at this time. This is the time when the kitten learns how to be a cat. During play they learn to hunt, establish territory, and defend themselves. They learn to wash and groom themselves and each other, and to cover their wastes in the litter box. They learn the social graces and all the body language cats use to express themselves.

A kitten of four weeks is extremely appealing and

much easier to sell or to have adopted—there's no denying that. But such kittens, separated too soon from the mother, are often the ones who develop behavioral or personality problems later on. The best plan is to allow prospective owners to come see the litter when they are four or five weeks old. They can choose a kitten and he can then be marked in the armpit with a drop of food coloring. (The color must be renewed twice a week because the mother usually licks it off.) The adoptive owner can then visit the kitten as much as he wants, the more the better. In fact, owner and kitten will get to know each other and the owner will have the immense satisfaction of witnessing how his kitten is getting the best possible start in life. Anyone who agrees with this plan would seem to be a person who sincerely has the welfare of the kitten at heart.

I also advised composing a list of requirements for the new owner. This serves as a means of teaching the new owners and can often prevent a tragedy. For example, you may take for granted that owners will have screens in windows to protect the cat from falling, or that they will have the cat neutered or spayed after he or she is mature. However, I know from long experience that not everyone considers such things important. Whenever I am asked to help with an adoption, be it for kittens or mature cats, I always have the new owner read and sign two copies of an agreement with a list of adoption requirements—one copy for the adoptive owner and one for me.

My own adoption agreement contains prohibitions against declawing and allowing the cat to run unsupervised outdoors, as well as dietary requirements, a promise of a yearly visit to the veterinarian, and visiting privileges for me during the first month and at least twice a year thereafter. The last requirement on the list is a promise that, if for any reason the owner cannot continue to keep the cat himself, the cat must be returned to me and to no one else. I, in turn, promise to accept the cat. This insures the cat's safety, which sets everyone's mind at rest. It also lets the new owner feel that he or she is getting an animal who is loved and cherished.

Making up their list helped to prepare the Di Pietros' minds to evaluate prospective owners. They felt much more relaxed about the adoptions after I proposed that they could do as I do and stipulate that the first month is a trial period for everyone, the cats included. This acknowledges that human beings can make a mistake and that mistakes can be corrected.

Several times I have had cats returned to me because a cat already in the home did not get along with the new cat. I try to help owners realize that, when dealing with living creatures, one never knows for sure how an adoption will work out. To say "it's not working" after a couple of weeks of sincere effort does *not* mean you have failed. The mistake would be to try to force an unsuitable relationship.

The following week, when the kittens were about four weeks old, I showed the Di Pietros how to wean them. As Louie and Angela led me downstairs, I realized that I would be very sorry to see this litter grow up and leave. I was enjoying my weekly visits and the Di Pietros were spoiling me with Mamma Di Pietro's special dishes.

When Louie, Angela, and I entered the storeroom, we found the whole brood out in the middle of the floor. A bushel basket was turned over on its side and the kittens were having the time of their lives in, out and on top of it; clambering and falling, hissing and squeaking with pleasure as it rolled from side to side. Piccola was seated close by, proudly erect, her tail curled sedately around her feet.

All young kittens have a play-nurse-sleep cycle. For our first weaning session we had purposely chosen a time about twenty minutes before the kittens would normally nurse and sleep. Weaning is best done when the kittens are hungry. The best formula to use is a puree consistency—easy to scoop up on a finger and easy to lap. It should be a highly nutritious and digestable mixture, such as my Weaning Formula (see Appendix A) which Angela had prepared.

I waited until a couple of kittens began to tire and toddle towards Piccola, expecting to nurse. Then we put two big, flat dinner plates down on the floor with four little piles of weaning formula on each, a total of eight portions. It is a good idea to set a couple of extra places to insure that no one will complicate the lesson by crowding or pushing. Also, it helps a lot if the mother will come and eat first, providing a model for the little ones to follow, so a place should be set for her as well.

The method is this: the owner dips his finger into the food and holds the food under a kitten's nose for the kitten to smell. The owner then touches the food lightly to the kitten's nose, leaving a dot of food clinging just above the upper lip. The kitten automatically licks the food off his nose, tastes how delicious it is, and, being hungry, looks for more. Again present your finger below the nose and, this time, on smelling the food, the kitten will stick his nose into it to gain the satisfaction of licking it off. Now, while that little tongue is licking, the owner touches the food on his finger to the tongue so that the kitten finds himself licking the finger instead of his nose. This is a big step. Now, continue to dip your finger into the food and let the kitten lick it off. Keep moving the finger closer to the plate, making the kitten reach for it so that each fingerful brings him closer to the plate. In the end, your finger should be submerged within the pile of food on the plate. Then you simply slide the finger away while the kitten continues to lap from the plate.

If you are so unwise as to allow all the kittens access to the plates at one time what follows is likely to be something like this. When the weaning formula is dished onto the two big plates, the inviting aroma will bring all the kittens as well as the mother scampering over. You will probably prove insufficient to the task of controlling the stampede, and at least three kittens will attain the center of the plates, wading through the food at the perimeter. If you do succeed in snatching one or two out and begin cleaning their paws, two more will surely get the idea and join the others in the center of the plates. All the kittens will probably agree, at this point, that the delicious-smelling goo underfoot would make a fine meal and, as every kitten knows, the only way to eat is by licking and sucking on another cat. So they will very probably all lay down right where they are and begin licking each other. Although you will have accomplished the successful introduction of the weaning formula into the kittens' lives, I think you will have to agree one kitten at a time is much better.

Don't insist that all the kittens learn on the first

day. Just let them all try, then keep repeating the lesson during the three or four feedings a day, and one by one they'll catch on. After four or five days, increase the weaning formula to four meals and finally five or six meals by the time the kittens are six weeks old and stop nursing altogether.

The six small meals will become four larger meals a day when the kitten is twelve weeks old. At five months you can cut down to three meals, and at seven months the kitten can begin the normal two meals a day. Of course, the schedule will vary slightly with the individual cat, so an owner must be sensitive to his own kitten's rhythm of growth and make adjustments accordingly.

More frequent feedings are needed when the kitten is small because now he is growing the fastest. He must meet the body's demand for the nutrients required to manufacture larger and larger bones and muscles. But, though his needs are large, his stomach is small. He cannot take in all he requires except by eating frequent, small, high-quality meals. Also, a young kitten's metabolism is lightning fast at this time. He will digest and use the food quickly and be hungry again soon. Feeding him too much at once will have two negative results. The stomach will stretch and produce an unattractive figure in later life, and overcrowding the stomach will prevent proper digestion of the food and cause it to pass through his system before the nutrients are absorbed.

The Di Pietros' kittens were star pupils. Piccola set a perfect example, daintily lapping at one small mound of puree. Then, one by one, her kittens went through the little training ritual and joined their mother around the plates. Angela weaned the little gray and white kitten gently and smoothly. The last was the little tortoise-shell, and she was for big Louie, kneeling over the plate, his brow creased in concentration, his finger almost as big as the kitten's whole head. When her tongue began licking at his big fingertip, Louie's face lit up like a Christmas tree, marveling at the little mite's intelligence.

I stopped Angela from offering seconds on this first meal. I wanted the kittens to nurse a bit and mix the old diet with the new. If change is too abrupt, diarrhea can result, and diarrhea in kittens is a serious matter. Before I left I cautioned the Di Pietros to repeat the whole weaning ritual, one kitten at a time, for the next two or three feedings, just to be sure, and to prevent messy feet. Brilliant as they were, I reminded Louie, they were still very young kittens.

Early the following week I was surprised to get a phone call from Louie reporting that Spats had pushed open the door to the storeroom and gone downstairs. It was, after all, part of his territory and he had a healthy curiosity about new and interesting smells coming from down there.

"Ya never saw anything like this, Anitra. That Piccola Mamma, she stood up real stiff, and her hair was all standing out, and I'm telling ya, I never heard her make a noise like that before. I mean, she sounded like she was so mad she was sort of garglin' and chokin' at the same time. Ya know what I mean?"

I knew. A female protecting her litter is a foe fearsome enough to make even a large dog turn tail and run. The sound Louie described is the deep-throated final warning given in a hostile encounter before raw rage overcomes the cat and a battle to the death ensues. I have heard the sound only a few times in my life, and that was a few times too many.

"What happened, Louie?" I tried not to sound too worried. "Is everything all right?"

"Ya shoulda been there, Anitra. Ya shoulda seen Spats."

"Well, what happened, Louie? Are they all right?"

"Oh yeah, they're fine. But ya shoulda seen what Spats done."

"Well, what did he do, for heaven's sake, tell me!"

"He didn't do nothin'. Ya know what I mean."

(No, I didn't.)

"Boy, I never saw nobody handle a female like that. Ya know what he done?"

(No, not yet, but I had patience.)

"She's standin there, see, makin' that noise. And Spats, he just comes on down the stairs pretendin' like he don't see her or nothin', ya know. He just walks right on by and over to me, just as cool as ya please. An' then ya know what he does?"

(Not yet.)

"He just lies down on the floor like he got tired and he's not even lookin' at her. Then he starts lickin' his chest. How d'ya like that? He's lyin' there washin' himself, and she's standing there yellin' at nothin. Ya ever heard-a anything like that?"

Yes, that I had. It sounded as if Spats had pulled the same routine that I used earlier, calming Piccola's fears by observing the very best feline etiquette. He had evidently decided he liked her looks, and he didn't want to fight her. So he chose an action that would buy him some time and give the lady a chance to cool down. "When in doubt, wash." Spats was no fool.

"Spats is a wise and clever cat, Louie. He was showing Piccola, by his actions, that he was no danger to her or the kittens. By washing himself he was giving her a chance to look him over. He probably finds her attractive."

There was a moment of silence from Louie while he put the information together with the scene he had witnessed.

"Anitra, I think ya got somethin' there." He lowered his voice conspiratorially. "Because Piccola, she changed her tune after she got a good look at him. Ya know what I mean? She didn't make no more noises. As a matter of fact, she also starts washin' herself too; just like she wants everybody to forget the whole thing."

"Louie," I said, "who could resist Spats?"

By the time Thursday dinner rolled around, Piccola Mamma had accepted Spats and Spats in turn had adopted the whole family. For as long as the kittens were there, he was Uncle Spats, teaching them the fine points of feline tag and wrestling. Yet he never missed a night up in the restaurant, carrying out his usual duties with the same impeccable style as always. Spats was a cat of many talents.

The big news the following week was the mouse. Wednesday morning, when Angela brought the food down, Piccola walked over, proud as punch, and dropped a dead mouse at her feet. Angela was at first startled to discover that there were any mice at all in their carefully kept storeroom, and then pleased that her little Piccola had presented herself as the solution along with the problem.

"Cats have a lot of pride," I explained over dinner that Thursday. "She's showing you that she likes you and she wants to repay you."

"And that bum Spats, he just sits there. Look at him, Anitra." Louie nodded toward the cash register where two men, one elderly and one middle-aged, were deep in conversation with their favorite *maitre d'*.

Spats, of course, was never one for just sitting around. He played a very important role in getting all five kittens adopted.

It was Angela who decided that if a customer was fond of Spats, he could probably be trusted with a kitten. So, one by one, selected individuals and families were informed that there were five kittens for adoption and then invited down to the storeroom to see them. Since Spats always seized any excuse to visit the storeroom, he always led the way down, woke the kittens, and got them rolling and tussling in their most engaging fashion. Everyone naturally assumed they were Spat's kittens, and the Di Pietros neither confirmed nor denied the rumor. Louie would just nod and smile, then abruptly change the subject. The upshot was that since everyone who visited was a customer who adored Spats, they all wanted Spats's kittens.

Piccola was spayed shortly after the last kitten was adopted. Then she returned to the restaurant to accept a permanent position as Supervisor of Mousing—under Spats, of course.

RALPH'S STORY

JAMES FRANKIS VAX   CRIS ARBO

CHAPTER THREE

SRALPH'S STORY
The Rambunctious Months: 8 Weeks to 8 Months

FROM the time the kitten first attains full command of his body until he passes through sexual maturity, his exuberant activity will test the tolerance of the entire household. I call this period "the rambunctious months" because Nature has programmed this stage of a kitten's life as the time of wild abandon. He will scamper and leap and jump about like a young jackrabbit for what seem like impossibly long and frenzied sessions. He will then abruptly stop and flop over like a discarded bean bag and sleep like the dead, often in the middle of a busy room. If your kitten acts like this, he is only following Nature's dictates and exercising his growing body to the limits. He is building strength and endurance.

The kitten is irresistibly adorable at this stage, but it may seem to an inexperienced owner that his bundle of fluff has turned out to be rather more of a handful than he'd bargained for. That is why I often suggest adopting a settled-down adult cat, whose body is developed and whose personality is formed. Of course, many people *insist* on having a kitten, and this is fine as long as they are prepared to undertake the extra precautions and feeding requirements needed by the very young.

I already had three adult cats in residence when a very young kitten entered our lives.

"Hola Señora! You want a kitten?" Little Rosario Paz stepped off the curb in front of our building just as my bike glided up. I hit the brakes and dismounted. My young neighbor was thrusting towards me a little black and white kitten which he had suspended under the armpits, hindquarters dangling. "His name is Cap-i-tan Kirk."

"Of the Starship Enterprise," I responded without thinking. "Marooned on an alien planet, is he?"

Little Captain Kirk, looking perfectly content, gave a small kick with one hind foot and set himself swinging gaily. My attention was captured by the large number of fleas promenading in and out among the sparse white hairs of the kitten's pink belly. Rosario pulled the kitten in to belt level, rear end still dangling, and I pulled my attention away from the flea colony and back to the child.

"Where did he come from, Rosario?"

"He is living behind in the alley for a long time, Señora. He don't belong to nobody." The youngster's eyes pleaded behind the unfamiliar English words.

The kitten was about six or seven weeks old. Rosario presented him again, and I thought of my own three cats upstairs. The last thing we needed was a flea-ridden kitten.

Rosario's eyes kept darting apprehensively across the street. "Cap-i-tan Kirk, he cannot stay here no more, Señora. Lupo Ramirez is coming with his big dog. He like to hunt the cats."

I assumed that Lupo Ramirez must be the older boy from across the street who owned the athletic-looking Alaskan malamute.

I looked at the bright shoe-button eyes and the tiny pink nose of Cap-i-tan Kirk and remembered the size and energy of that dog.

An occupational hazard for a cat groomer is that everybody in the neighborhood turns to you whenever there's a cat in need. I was caught this time and I knew it. What kind of a citizen would I be if I didn't encourage kindness to animals in this child? Anyway, the groomer in me was dying to get those horrendous fleas off of that kitten's adorable pink skin.

"Okay, Rosario." I reached for the kitten and lifted him onto my shoulder, where he crouched and clung like a little limpet, digging his needle claws into my wool jacket. "We can't let Captain Kirk be eaten by an alien monster, can we? I'll try to find a good safe home for him."

The boy's face lit up. "He is a verry good cat, Señora, you will like him."

He skipped along beside the bike and held the door for me as I carried little Captain Kirk into the safety of the building. I turned to thank Rosario, but he had already darted away into the street.

"You can come up and visit him sometime if you want to," I called after him.

My cats smelled the kitten the minute I opened the door. Nose tips tilted up at me and whiskers trembled with quick little inhalations as three curious cats drew in the messages of Captain Kirk's scents. Purr, Florence, and Priscilla were used to my coming home covered with the scents of strange cats. They were not used to my walking in carrying a kitten on my shoulder.

Captain Kirk, for his part, showed for the first time some surprise at what the world had to offer. He clamped himself harder and flatter, digging in his claws to make sure he wouldn't tumble down into that awesome crowd of big cat creatures. The poor little thing had probably been living alone in the alley for so long, he'd all but forgotten what another cat looked like. He must really have felt he was on an alien planet.

I didn't pause, but continued on through the apartment. "I have a special surprise for you tonight," I caroled, "but let's have some dinner first." And with that I whisked the kitten into the bathroom, closing the door behind me.

Introducing a new cat to the family is always best made when tummies are full and the cats are contented. I would also have to trim all the cats' nails, just as a precaution.

While the three adult cats were dining in the living room, Captain Kirk spent the dinner hour quite happily in the dry bathtub. Let the flea eggs drop where they may; I would simply wash out the tub after I got the kitten cleaned up.

I watched little Captain Kirk dig into his own small

portion. Captain Kirk—the name didn't fit. A cat should be thoughtfully named. By itself, a name is a tool of communication. Cats can sense our mental attitudes, and every time we say a name or, for that matter, any word, corresponding pictures and emotions are called forth in our minds. By choosing the right name we can influence what those pictures and emotions will be and consequently, what the cat will "pick up" every time he hears his name. A name can help to mold a cat's personality. For example, a cat who takes offense easily and attacks others or hisses at humans would do well with a name like Teddy, because to humans it calls forth thoughts of cuddling and purring, which will be communicated to the cat. A shy cat needs a name that inspires respect, like Alexander or, for a female, Princess.

This little cutie, who was practically inhaling his food in my bathtub, didn't have any personality problems, so I had *carte blanche* to name him anything that was complimentary and uplifting.

He finished the last smidgen of gravy, looked up, and began to try to climb up the side of the tub to me. I slid my palm under his belly and lifted him up in front of my face. Why not a name that sounded like what he was. A small, friendly name—Ralph.

"Ralph?" I said, and he wiggled out of my hand and onto my shoulder again.

"Ra-alph," I crooned, as he snuggled into my neck, and began nuzzling my ear lobe.

"I'll call you Ralph for now, and then your new owner can name you whatever he or she likes after you're adopted." I hoped it would be soon. I didn't want to become too attached.

I replaced Ralphie in the tub, so I could get his flea bath ready. It was then that I noticed the rickets. His shaky little hind legs were quite bowed, showing that his diet had been lacking in calcium and vitamin D, and heaven knows what else. Whatever Rosario and the other kids had been feeding him in the alley, it had obviously not been nutritious enough for a growing kitten.

I mixed another teaspoon of the same homemade food my cats were enjoying with one-quarter teaspoon each of cod liver oil, which is high in vitamin D, and bone meal, a good source of calcium. Ralph pounced on it and did his vacuum cleaner routine again.

It's a big temptation to feed a starving kitten too much. Don't do it. He'll either vomit the whole thing up or, even worse, you'll stretch the stomach and the kitten will have poor digestion and an unattractive figure for life.

After dinner little Ralph had his bath in a mixing bowl. Drowned fleas floated in gray bath water and disappeared down the drain while Ralph tried to convince me that it was high time we left these damp environs for drier ground.

Fleas can carry tapeworm, so I made a mental note to collect a stool sample and take it to the veterinarian to be examined under the microscope. Ralph acquiesced to a thorough rinsing, and in less than fifteen minutes the whole job was finished and Mister Pink Nose was wrapped snuggly in a dishtowel and ready for the blow dryer. Being so small and sparsely furred, I had him fluffed in short order and ready to meet the rest of the family.

Introduction of a new cat to the household should

usually be done by someone the family cats don't know. It should proceed in a formal and orderly manner to insure a smooth transition period while the new and the old get to know one another.

But my cats are used to the comings and goings of cats coming in to be groomed and sick cats boarding for special diets and nursing care, so I just marched out to the center of the room with the kitten, placed him on the floor, and turned and walked away as if I didn't care a hoot what happened to him.

It was Purr's nose that reached forward first and began taking stock of the new arrival. Priscilla and Florence, my Siamese mother-and-daughter team, perched safely atop the big armchair sending huffy little hisses of disapproval in my direction.

Ralph cowered on the hardwood floor, a trembling little ball of anxiety watching Big Purr move in toward him. Purr was concentrating entirely on the odors emanating from the kitten—odors of cat, of fear, of shampoo, of Anitra, and of nasty cod liver oil! Should he reject or accept?

While he hovered in this state of indecision (Purr is not a decisive cat), the kitten, overcome with apprehension, flipped over onto his back and began wiggling frantically about, skinny hind legs pumping the air, until he had twisted himself around so that his soft pink tummy was directly under Big Purr's nose.

What could Purr do? The baby had instinctively taken the age–old "position of submission." Every species has in its body language a posture that renders it un-attackable and inviolable by others of its species. Thus Nature protects its young and defenseless.

Big Purr's response was instinctive. The kitten's

posture, a powerful message of helpless vulnerability, had overridden all the other messages Purr had picked up. Here was an unthreatening, defenseless baby who was, he decided upon consulting his nose again, afraid and smelling horribly from cod liver oil. Well, one thing was sure: If this kitten was going to lie around on Big Purr's floor, he would certainly have to be cleaned up. So, with nose crinkling in disgust, he began to ply his large and prickly tongue to Ralph's head and face, cleaning away the offensive residue.

Now, this was an experience a kitten could remember well! Ralph wiggled and squeaked and kicked with glee until, with a final sweep of his tongue, Big Purr had flipped him back onto his feet and was strolling disdainfully away across the floor, licking the foul mess off his own teeth and gums. In worshipful silence the little one watched him go. Then, clean, full, and overcome with drowsiness, he curled himself into a tight little black and white ball and fell asleep right where he was, in the middle of the living room floor. Throughout the foregoing scene, we had been treated to intermittant soft hisses of disapproval and distaste from Florence on the back of the arm chair, and Priscilla now down on the end table.

Little Mr. Pink Nose was so easygoing and innocent he soon bumbled his way into the hearts of my three adult cats. In Purr I was very lucky to have an adult cat who would take over the kitten's training. Kittens of this age must be taught wrestling, tag, soccer, attack, escape, hiding, climbing, and stalking, as well as the finer skills of personal cleanliness and feline etiquette, to prepare them for a normal life of interaction with other cats and with humans. Quite a plateful for a kitten no bigger than a man's fist.

For my part, I would not be able to close a drawer without checking inside or slam a door behind me without looking, and I had to adopt the "kitten owner's shuffle." This is a method of locomotion closely akin to cross-country skiing, without the skis, in which you slide your feet along the floor, never really lifting them completely so that you never run the risk of crushing a scampering paw with your heavy heel or toes. Kittens have complete and total trust in the safety of their world; that's why so many of them don't make it through their first year. Mother Nature prepared them to survive in the wild. She didn't prepare them for quickly moving high-heeled shoes or big clumping boots. Nor did Nature give them any defense against slamming doors and drawers, which can break tiny bones and injure or kill a trusting kitten. Once you adopt a kitten, or even an adult cat, you can never again slam a door behind you without looking first to be sure the coast is clear. An accident leaves a terrible scar on the mind of the owner, even if there is no permanent damage to the cat or kitten. This is one of the many reasons I do not advise getting a kitten for a child. Older cats are wiser and less likely to get hurt if a child forgets and lets a door slam carelessly behind him.

Kittens can also be accidently trapped inside places. Their noses lead them to explore an interesting odor inside a closet or drawer; they fall asleep, and someone comes along and closes them in. Usually the family soon misses the kitten and searches him out before he becomes frightened or something worse happens. But sometimes soon isn't quick enough. The odors from the open refrigerator or the delightful warmth inside the clothes dryer can lure a kitten to certain death. So always look before you slam.

I wanted this kitten to be both healthy and easy to care for—in other words, eminently adoptable. So, besides feeding him my basic diet (see Appendix A) and adding a quarter-teaspoon of bone meal and cod liver oil to each meal, I also began establishing desirable behavior patterns.

Nature gives all young creatures the ability to learn easily. But they forget easily too, so the best approach is to first establish desirable behavior patterns and then stick to them over the first three months or so. The repetition will then establish the pattern firmly in the kitten's mind. For example, if you don't want the cat on the dining table or the kitchen counter, never let the kitten get up there. Not even once. If you vary the pattern, you'll only confuse the cat.

Another example: I keep very irregular hours, and I don't want the cats to wake me up in the morning because they want to be fed. So I make sure that I never, never feed the cats the minute I get up. I don't want them to associate my getting up with their being fed. So, I insert several activities in between. First I brush my teeth, start the breakfast, clean the litter boxes; only then do I feed the cats.

Such cat care activities as being groomed, having nails clipped, riding in the carry case, and taking pills can all be pleasant and comfortable if they are properly presented and handled. Every day I made sure to pet Ralph all over. I would slowly and gently stroke the inside as well as the outside of his ears. I would pet his feet and extrude each claw by pressing up on the pad. I even stroked his gums and teeth. Since no one had ever told him that this was odd, he accepted it and enjoyed it the same as any other petting and stroking.

Kittens learning about their bodies use their claws the way human babies chew when they're teething. Kittens love to try their claws all over creation—but this doesn't last. Just like a baby's teething, it's only a phase they go through, and then they decide that the scratching post feels best of all.

It is during the adolescent clawing period that owners sometimes make the mistake of allowing a cat to be declawed. Perhaps these people are not aware that the kitten is just going through a phase—and it *will* pass. Or perhaps they don't know that a cat or kitten needs a *rough* scratching surface. If they provide a rough scratchy scratching post, one which is not wobbly, then that is where the cat will scratch. Most owners never dream that the declawing operation is, in reality, ten amputations and that it is horribly painful after the cat wakes up from the anesthetic. It never occurs to them that declawing is in reality removing all of the cat's toes, turning him into a "club foot," and that this will affect the cat's balance, muscular development, and emotional security for the rest of his life.

While it is extremely important for a young cat like Ralph to scratch in order to develop his growing body, adult cats too need to scratch to tone the muscles of the forelegs, shoulders and back. A cat's scratching post must be secure so that it doesn't tip over or wobble the minute the cat starts to scratch, and it should be two and a half or three feet tall so he can really stretch out and reach for the top. Most importantly, it must be harsh and scratchy like the back of a carpet.

It's fairly easy to correct a problem scratching post. If a post wobbles and threatens to tip over, it can be laid on its side. If it's not "scratchy" enough, it can be re-covered with a piece of carpet, back side out. I prefer the Felix Katnip Tree post because it's made of sisal and saturated with catnip. (See Appendix C for ordering information.)

To encourage Ralph to use the post instead of the furniture, I had to associate it with happy occasions, such as mealtime or my arrival home. So, at these times I would begin scratching the post myself. Ralph soon got used to my "greeting ritual" which included my own scratch on the post whenever I returned home. Then he and the other cats would follow my lead and I would stop scratching the post to pet them, and give each one personal attention.

Ralph also loved the carry case. And why not? It was a fun place to receive a treat or to jump in and out of while pursuing a toy or a knotted cord. A kitten is open to all suggestions as to how life should be lived. If I demonstrated that rubbing the gums and the inside of the cheek feels good or that the carry case was a perfectly delightful conveyance, he had no reason to doubt me. I congratulated myself that I was creating a superadoptable kitten. I fed him in the bathroom away from the others, since he was getting a kitten's allowance of four to six meals a day and the others only two. Also, I had to be sure that his extra dietary supplements would not be appropriated by Florence. Unlike Purr, she dotes on cod liver oil. Florence gets her own ration—to eat the kitten's as well would be too much of a good thing.

Our little one began filling out, but not too much. Shaping up might be a better way of putting it. Every day Uncle Purr conducted training maneuvers all over the apartment, chasing across the window sills and over the furniture—Purr in the lead and, later, Purr trailing behind. A kitten has more energy than you or I could ever dream possible. Uncle Purr soon began to "shape up" as well.

I knew that Ralph's exuberance would continue and even increase until shortly after he was neutered, at about seven or eight months. At that time he would be nearly grown and his glands would be ready to settle down to their normal life functions. To neuter too soon prevents normal development of the cat and can cause physical problems later on. It is fairly easy to tell when the cat has matured and the proper time for neutering has arrived, because the urine of the mature male cat begins to smell quite strongly and quite different from that of a kitten or a female cat. If the mature male is left unneutered, he usually settles down all right anyway, but he also begins to spray all around his territory, so if you didn't notice a distinctive smell before, you certainly will at this point. I would have to see that the new owner knew to watch for the signs of maturity and see that the operation was done.

For now I thanked my lucky stars that Purr was on the job keeping Mr. Pink Nose busy. But even Purr had to rest sometime. Then Ralph would go scampering off to continue his very thorough explorations of every nook and cranny of his small universe. With Purr asleep, I would be the one who would have to be on the job if I didn't want spilled waste baskets and unrolled toilet paper. It was during this period that Ralph came to believe that "Ralph" was actually his last name. He thought his first name was Dammit, as in "Dammit, Ralph, get down out of there!"

But in spite of, or maybe partly because of all this,

I loved having a kitten in the house. I loved the racing and the tumbling and the end of the chase when Big Purr would grapple Ralph into his chest and hold him there while he rolled the two of them over and over, protecting Ralph from harm with his own big body and strong legs. I was alarmed at first, for it really looked as if Big Purr was going to squash the little fellow under him; but then I saw the look on Ralph's face. It reminded me of a kid on his first roller coaster ride. They always contrived to end their tussles this way, and then the two of them would settle down on my sleeping mat for a mutual wash. If Ralph didn't clean himself to Purr's satisfaction, Purr would take his own prickly tongue to him, holding Ralph down with a forepaw until he was through.

After the cleanup came nap time. Kittens are experts at molding themselves to another cat's body; snuggling was the one thing that Ralph could do better than anybody else. He was healthy, adorable, and wonderfully tractable. Now, where was I going to find an owner for this paragon?

Of all the potential owners in New York, I would never have thought of Augusta Michaels, had she not made the suggestion herself. For as long as I had known her, and as much as I liked her, I had never ever thought of her as a likely candidate to adopt a cat, much less a kitten. She was a retired English teacher who had taught in a junior high school for girls, "back in the days when all proper young ladies went to a girls' school," she would declare, peering at me over her bifocals.

I first met her at the Beauty Alcove, where I called

every month to groom Chantilly and Butch, Monsieur Armand's two gorgeous Persians. Our standing appointments always seemed to coincide with Miss Michaels' wash and set. She would always be there, perched on the big antique barber's chair and draped in one of Monsieur Armand's voluminious pink and red smocks.

She would often remark on her great good fortune at finding a hairdresser in the very same building where she lived. "And such a clever one too," she would add, beaming up at Monsieur Armand as he arranged her hair into precise gray waves which ended in a neat braided bun at the nape of her neck.

I judged her to be in her seventies and since she could not "get about" as easily as she once had, she carried a slim black cane which she would sometimes use to punctuate her conversation, sweeping it about or making little pokes at the floor.

Augusta liked to get me talking about the cats I had worked on during the past month. She was a most appreciative audience, urging me on to divulge further details about the private lives of my feline friends. I was surprised when she told me she had never owned a pet. But she explained that until recently she had had a very busy social life, including frequent adventures with her young grandnephew who had recently entered junior high school. I could tell that Augusta was a little lonely.

Then, one afternoon while I was combing out Chantilly, Augusta got me launched into a portrayal of "El Cap-i-tan Kirk's" adventures in the alley with Rosario Paz and his narrow escape from the "big dog of Lupo Ramirez." I was rewarded by several appreciative chortles from Monsieur Armand but, from Augusta, only one gasp of horror when I mentioned the rickets.

She sat quietly for the rest of the story. Then she nodded decisively and said, "I think I would very much like to adopt that little orphan and give him the home he deserves."

Taken completely by surprise, my comb stopped in midstroke; so did Monsieur Armand's. "A-goos-*ta!*" he wailed. "What of your beautiful *jardin* with the so adorable little birds, *alors!*" Augusta lived in the garden apartment at the end of the hall.

Most New York gardens are little more than glorified driveways fenced off from the main alley. But Augusta had a *real* garden, with a small mimosa tree in one corner, to shade the birdbath and feeders. Her garden had acquired such repute among the feathered transients that Augusta had counted fifty-four species of bird visitors over the years.

My reaction to her sudden decision to turn from cat story listener to participant was not much better than Monsieur Armand's. Somehow I couldn't quite picture prim Augusta carrying a heavy bag of litter or setting a placemat on the floor, much less surviving the rambunctious months.

But although a kitten might not be a good choice for her, I had to agree that she did need a cat. I knew of three adult cats who were up for adoption who would suit her just fine.

Senior citizens need what I call a trouble-free cat. All three cats that I had in mind were just that—mixed-breed short-hairs over three years old. They had all been neutered, and because they were short-hairs, they were easy to groom. Being mixed breeds, they enjoyed

robust good health with none of the congenital weaknesses that can show up in pure-bred cats. None had
been declawed, so they were calm with no excessive
aggressiveness or timidity, and there were no problems
of balance and no weak shoulder and back muscles.
All three were "people cats" as opposed to "cat's
cats"—that is, they were oriented toward communication with people. Any one of them would be perfect
for a senior citizen who could not "get about" as well
as she used to.

I described each one and then suggested that I take
Augusta around to visit them so she could choose for
herself. But Augusta had made up her mind; she had
her heart set on "that poor little mite with the rickets."
I had told the story too well.

"I am not in my dotage quite yet, Armand," she
said, cutting his protests short. "Even if there were no
birds in my garden, I would certainly not allow a cat
to run loose out of doors! I know quite well about the
dangers of poisonings and kidnappers and roaming
Tom cats." Augusta had not been listening to my cat
stories in vain for the past three years. She had a mind
like a steel trap.

Augusta settled back into the chair and Armand and
I communicated with a glance over the top of Augusta's
waved hair. I shook my head and Armand rolled his
eyes heavenward as he always did when Augusta became adamant.

If someone asks to adopt a cat I might not have
chosen for them—and they insist—I usually go along
with it. You never can tell. I have seen what appeared
to be impossible combinations work out smoothly. So
my adoption procedure always begins with a one-

month trial period and weekly visits from me. It was agreed that I would bring the kitten over the following Sunday.

If I could get her through the next five or six months, it just might work out. But, oh, those next five or six months! I would soon find out what sort of stuff Miss Augusta Michaels was made of.

It was a warm Sunday evening when little Ralph, peering through the transparent dome of my smallest carry case, got his first look at the brand-new universe that was to be his home. Augusta's apartment was an ideal place for a cat. She had done a thorough job of cat-proofing before our arrival by having screens put in all the windows. And she had closed off the larger room, which also served as the kitchen, so that her new kitten would have a comfortably small space in which to begin establishing territory.

I sat on a big square cushion on the floor and opened up the case. Ralph looked as if he thought he had landed on yet another alien planet. He was as tense as a field mouse, sniffing and looking and listening all at once. There were so many new sounds and odors, and no other cats around to tell him which were safe and which were not.

We didn't rush him. Augusta brewed tea, we talked and, after ten minutes, I lifted him out of his case and let him sit beside me on the floor. Augusta and I continued to talk casually, and watched him as he slowly and carefully began to explore the fascinating new scents that were beguiling his nose from all directions.

Augusta was naturally polite in a way that appeals to cats. She waited for him to come to her in his own good time and then greeted him cordially as he sniffed her proffered finger. "You make yourself at home, my dear," she murmured smilingly, "and we'll have a nice little snack later on."

During the course of his explorations he came running back periodically as if to touch base with me, his source of security. When he began to include Augusta in this little ritual we knew he had accepted her as a human he could trust.

When he went into the bathroom alone and used the litter box, Augusta was triumphant. "There now, Anitra, you see? He is perfectly at home here already." We listened to him expertly scratching the litter, exactly as he had been taught by his Uncle Purr.

Augusta beamed as her new kitten returned to the room again. "I'm so pleased his name is Ralph," she confided, peering over her bifocals. "After Emerson, isn't it?"

"After . . .?" I coughed to cover my confusion. "Emerson, Emerson," yes, I nodded enthusiastically. "Ralph Waldo Emerson, the philosopher. Suits him, doesn't it?"

For the next couple of weeks Augusta called me each day and left a "Ralph Report" on my telephone answering machine. She knew I would be interested in his progress and she enjoyed sharing his escapades with me. As I had predicted, her chief problem was channeling that boundless energy.

When I visited next, I watched one of Ralph's favorite feats—jumping from the chair onto Augusta's shoulder. "I hope he doesn't use his claws," I remarked, remembering that first night when a terrified Mr. Pink Nose clung to the shoulder of my jacket.

"Oh my, no," she laughed, "as long as I move

steadily he can keep his balance quite easily without using his claws." I watched as she sat down on the chair and a sedate Ralph stepped gracefully from his perch. "Ralph," she laughed, "are you going to make an athlete out of me, or am I going to make a philosopher out of you?" Augusta patted her knee and Ralph was in her lap and settled down in two seconds, a look of proprietary pleasure on his face.

Augusta was using every technique I could think of to drain his energy—cardboard boxes, paper bags, and finally a marvelous rope swing, knotted at the bottom, which dangled from a plant hook the janitor had anchored securely in the ceiling.

"It's supposed to hold fifty pounds," she assured me, "so I'm quite sure it's safe enough." Ralph jumped up and gripped the knotted end with all fours. Augusta gave the rope a firm push with her cane and set him swinging. Mr. Pink Nose was in kitten paradise.

At my suggestion, Augusta kept all the cat toys in a drawer and rotated them, giving him a "new" one twice a day so he would never tire of them. I had checked them out for kitten safety to be sure there was no thread or string or glued-on noses or anything else that a cat could swallow. Young Ralph's greatest favorite was a Ping-Pong ball that skittered and bounced crazily across the kitchen tiles.

Seated now in a big stuffed chair by the back windows, which looked out on the little garden, Augusta stroked Ralph's glossy back. He had fallen asleep almost instantly. "Just look at him," she turned to me, "he literally sleeps like the dead."

Kittens are a study in contrasts. Who would suspect that this little sleeping angel was the same kitten who enjoyed playing Tarzan on the rope and tobogganing throw rugs across the tiles. Augusta described how, at least twice a day he'd take a running start, make a flying leap, land in the center of the kitchen throw rug and go flying across the floor and crash into the opposite wall. And this was the kitten who once had rickets!

Augusta beamed proudly the first time I was on hand to witness the feat. "You see!" she exclaimed as she straightened the rug back into place with the tip of her cane, "he's really quite intelligent, Anitra. The use of tools requires a very highly developed mind, you know, and Ralph is definitely *using* this rug, don't you agree?" I did agree, very seriously and smiled inwardly. Young Ralph's adoption was going very well indeed.

I would have been even more delighted if I had known what was in store for him in the near future, for by mid-July that lovely garden of Augusta's included a protected play area for Ralph—an area that was completely safe because wire mesh enclosed it entirely. It covered the top and was embedded a foot into the ground. I always caution owners about letting their domestic cats out of doors due to the many potential dangers they can encounter, such as poisons, wild Tom cats, and other animals such as dogs and raccoons who might attack a trusting domestic animal.

Anyone can construct an enclosed outdoor play area with chicken wire or any serviceable screening or mesh. One needn't enclose the whole yard. Simply choose an area that includes grass, shade, sun, and perhaps a plant your cat enjoys nibbling, such as mint or catnip. There should be a litter box and water available too. If you can include the trunk of a tree in the

enclosure—or, even better, one or two lower branches—then you are definitely getting into the realm of
Cloud Nine.

Ralph's giant run was just high enough to allow
Augusta to stand erect. The far end was angled up and
securely anchored onto the high wooden fence, thus
including the two lower branches of the little mimosa
tree.

Ralph's second favorite spot in all the world was
the lower, thicker branch where he could sprawl like
a napping lion, one hind leg dangling. He loved to
birdwatch for hours on end. His first favorite spot, of
course, was Augusta's lap.

Since Ralph would be exposed to fleas outdoors, I
suggested some preventive measures. I had Augusta
add a tiny piece of crushed raw garlic to Ralph's food
every day and we made sure that the yeast in his Vita-
Mineral Mix was brewer's yeast. Also, every day before
he went out, Augusta would dust his coat all over with
brewer's yeast powder. Fleas don't like garlic or brewer's yeast, but Ralph certainly did. At three months he
was the picture of robust good health.

Augusta and I signed and exchanged copies of the
adoption agreement on the fourth Sunday after Ralph's
arrival. Augusta had expressed concern over the possibility that she might be unable to cope with Ralph's
care at some point in the future if anything should go
amiss with her own health, so she felt reassured by
my standard stipulations that she must keep me informed if Ralph ever fell ill and that, if ever she herself
could not care for him, he was to be returned to me
and to no one else. I would then either board him for

her for a while or personally supervise his placement in another good home.

The papers were signed to the accompanying creak of the rope swing as an exuberant Ralph demonstrated how the lashing of one's tail could both augment and prolong the ride. Augusta was right. Ralph was definitely a cat of unusual intelligence.

MAIZEY'S STORY

James Francis Fox

CRIS ARBO

CHAPTER FOUR

MAIZEY'S STORY

The Adult Cat Eight Months through Prime

MAIZEY landed in the animal shelter when she was four years old. Actually, she wasn't Maizey then; she didn't have a name. She was just a very puny little yellow Persian cat, one of a large group of unwanted cats brought in by the shelter's collection truck.

After a thorough examination by the veterinarian up on the third floor, they were each put into wire transporting cages the size of a small carrying case. A large man with big leather gloves then stacked the cages on a large pushcart, and Maizey and the others braced themselves, crouching in terror as they rattled and bumped down a series of ramps to the first-floor display area.

Maizey, like the rest of the cats, would be given three days in a display cage. On the evening of the third day, if she was not adopted, she would be brought back upstairs to the veterinary section to be destroyed by lethal injection.

When the cart stopped in the display room, the man picked up Maizey's cage, opened the door, and before she knew what was happening, a big leather glove grabbed her by the scruff of the neck. She was flipped onto her side and, with a skill gained from long practice, the man slipped her out and deposited her neatly in the large cage at the end. It already held four other long-haired cats of various colors.

Finding herself free to move about for the first time in several hours, Maizey darted to the back of the cage and wedged herself into the only shelter she could find—behind the litter box, up against the back wall. She pressed her body down against the floor and watched the man with the big leather gloves pulling forth the other cats and thrusting them into various cages.

Another movement caught her eye and she tried to compress herself into an even smaller ball behind the litter box. A lady with a clipboard was moving toward her cage. Past experience had taught Maizey that humans cannot be trusted. They are cruel, especially the little ones, the human kittens. They can squeeze a cat; they can pull and twist; her pupils dilated with terror. If only she could frighten the woman away. She took a deep breath, opened her mouth, and hissed as loud as she could.

"What about this fluffy yellow one?" the lady called to the man with the gloves as she looked from her clipboard into the cage.

As a volunteer worker she had been carefully filling out the cage cards for the new arrivals, telling the name, age, sex, and the reason why each cat was given up for adoption. The ten-year-old Burmese in the first cage had been calling for his owner nonstop all morning. His cage card read: "Bernie, Burmese, Male, 10 years—Family moved away." The card for the eight-year-old Siamese couple in the next cage stated: "Spouse dislikes cats." And so it went, all down the line: "Fiancée allergic," "Apartment too small," "Owner died," or, most often, simply, "Stray," "Stray," "Stray."

"Call it a stray," the big man shouted back, slamming the last cage door shut, and then he was gone, rattling his cart full of empty cages down the hall. He was a busy man. The shelter was overcrowded. But, then, the shelter was always overcrowded.

The lady volunteer wrote "Stray" on the card and slid it into the door slot. Maizey hissed again.

"I'm not going to hurt you, little one," the lady murmured and took a step back. "You'll have to calm down, baby, or nobody'll want to adopt you." And then she too was gone and the lights went out and the only sound left was Bernie the Burmese, still calling for his owner to come and take him home.

As luck would have it, Maizey's first full day in the display room was a Saturday, the busiest day of the week. She remained crouched behind the litter box, watching large numbers of humans come and stare and go away again. She had stopped hissing and simply tried to remain inconspicuous. In this she succeeded very well. Nobody wanted her; nobody even asked about her. She didn't eat, she didn't drink, and she didn't pass a stool. She did, however, urinate all over the floor and herself when the lady volunteer opened the cage and reached in to lift out the large black Persian male lounging by the water dish. When Maizey

saw that hand reaching in toward her, she was overcome with terror and lost control of her bladder. For
the rest of the day she crouched in the smelly puddle,
panting and trembling.

Bernie the Burmese resumed his calling as soon as
the first humans appeared, although his voice was becoming rather hoarse. By day's end several cats had
been adopted. A young couple who brought their own
carrying case took the two Siamese in the cage next to
Bernie's. The lady volunteer was beaming jubilant approval as she ushered them out the door. In the past
she had often been forced to break up such a pair.

"This Persian cage is a mess!" the cage boy who
cleaned up every night shouted from the other end of
the room.

The lady volunteer closed the door after the last of
the crowd, turned, and walked back.

"It's the little yellow one behind the box," she said,
shaking her head. "Poor creature, I honestly believe
it's better just to put them quietly to sleep when they're
so nervous. Now nobody'll want to take any of the Persians with the cage smelling like that. Just leave that
cage alone and I'll speak to Dr. Brody about the situation."

Then, once again, the lights went out and the shelter was quiet.

The second day, being Sunday, was much like the
first. Bernie the Burmese had given up calling for his
owner. He lay in a state of mourning with his head to
the wall until a plump little lady with white hair lifted
him gently, cradled him to her bosom, and exclaimed,
"Owners moved away! What do they mean, 'moved
away'!" Her blue eyes blinked indignantly and focused

on the lady volunteer. "And just left him behind, I suppose, like a piece of old crockery, did they!" Bernie began licking her chin. "Well, never you mind, little Bernie . . ." And smiling, the lady volunteer led the two of them out to the front desk.

Sunday evening, after two-and-a-half days of tension, fear, and the horror of being soiled, Maizey was approaching a state of collapse. Ordinarily such an animal would have been mercifully put to sleep, but this was a weekend, and on the weekend the shelter staff is down to a skeleton crew. So Maizey was left in the cage to be dealt with the following morning.

On Monday morning bright and early, a natty little man with a salt-and-pepper crewcut and wearing carefully pressed army fatigues strode through the shelter doors. Frederick Stanhope, of Stanhope Ltd., Interior Design, was looking for a cat.

A master of the tasteful understatement, Mr. Stanhope had just completed the decor of his own recently acquired Park Avenue penthouse apartment. However, he had become aware as he looked about his home at all those muted tones and subdued textures that there could indeed be such a thing as too much perfection. His home had indubitably achieved the very pinnacle of muted elegance. However, it occurred to him that if he should ever give a party in these surroundings, there was the very real danger that all his guests would fall asleep. The place was a monumental tranquilizer. It needed life; it needed movement; it needed warmth, interest . . . a cat! A cat would do it very nicely! Something in taupe, or possibly ecru, in the way of a soft texture to complement the gray marble fireplace. And so on Monday morning Frederick Stanhope began his search where the widest selection in town was to be found, at the public animal shelter.

We human beings are complex and interesting creatures. Our personalities are made up of many facets and layers, and we juggle these many parts of ourselves and use them or hide them as the occasion demands. Those of us who know cats are aware that a cat, most particularly an adult cat, tends to call forth from the owner's personality those hidden or unknown facets that he is hiding even from himself. Indeed, a first encounter with That Special Cat That Was Meant For You can be and often is a veritable adventure in expanded self-awareness. Moreover, when the human involved is a first-time cat owner, he very often discovers, to his amazement, a whole new person within himself.

Thus Frederick Stanhope, all unawares, marched in resolute fashion down the rows of cages full of appealing whites and blacks and grays, intent upon his search for the correct color and texture to compliment his decor. He stopped at the large cage at the end of the row, because among the six Persians within there was one the color of creamed corn. This was a possibility, not precisely what he had in mind, perhaps, but definitely a possibility.

He sniffed. What was that disgusting odor? Maizey was crouched down behind the litter box, pressing herself against the floor. Only her eyes and ears and the top of her back were visible to Frederick. He stepped forward to get a closer look and became aware that the creature was trembling like a leaf. Frederick looked about to discover who or what she was afraid of, but he was alone in the room. There was no one else there. Fascinated, he leaned closer, his nose barely an inch from the wire, whereupon the cat's pupils grew enormous. Looking him straight in the eye, she opened her mouth and hissed vehemently.

Frederick Stanhope was stunned. No one had ever spoken to him like that before, never in all his life.

It is at such moments of total surprise that a person's carefully crafted facade can suddenly crack and crumble away, revealing the altogether unsuspected persona beneath.

In a flash of compassionate intuition, Frederick sensed that it was he that this little yellow scrap was terrified of and that the reason had to do with something dreadful that had happened in her past. This tiny creature before him, all alone, friendless and trembling in the clutches of stark terror, had yet found the courage to hiss defiance in his face. Wasn't she magnificent! And what a deplorable mess! His nose wrinkled with distaste. How could they have let this gallant little creature sink to such a state! Oh, the degradation! Obviously no one had appreciated, had understood, had cared, by heaven, had cared!

And so Frederick Stanhope, gentleman designer, became Frederick Stanhope, knight on a white charger. Frederick had found his cat.

I found Mr. Stanhope's message on my answering machine early Monday evening. "This is Frederick Stanhope. Please call me about bathing a cat." He included his telephone number. Then he paused and added, "As soon as possible, please." The sound of that last "please" made me dial his number immediately.

Mr. Stanhope gave me a graphic description of

Maizey's "deplorable condition," and I agreed to come over about nine o'clock that night, after my last client. I don't usually like to begin a job that late, but when an owner tells me a cat has soiled himself with urine or stool, that means there's acid on the skin. It itches and burns, and I call that an emergency situation. Mr. Stanhope was relieved, grateful, and utterly charming, and I wondered as I hung up if this could be *the* Frederick Stanhope.

I'd heard of him, of course. His work often appeared on the covers of architectural design magazines. Articles about the man himself revealed that his clientele included royalty and were all of that genre whose refined tastes demanded that elegant understatement for which Frederick Stanhope was so famous. And this was the man who had just told me that he had adopted a cat from a public shelter who was soaked with urine, "because she was such a gallant little creature and exactly the right color." Interesting.

He lived on Park Avenue in one of those palatial affairs built in the 1920's to accommodate the cream of society. The lobby was a study in opulence; pink marble walls with ebony furnishings, and sporting a set of art deco elevator doors which would have been right at home in the Metropolitan Museum of Art.

The elevator hummed its way up to the penthouse, the doors slid away, and there stood Himself, crewcut, starched army fatigues, and a very worried look on his face.

"Oh, Miss Anitra, thank you for coming," he welcomed me and led the way toward the back of the apartment. "She's wedged herself behind the file cabinet in the den. Every time I go near her, she hisses."

The den was off the kitchen, and as I approached the file cabinet, I could hear an exhausted cat panting rapidly and hissing with every breath.

"They really didn't want to let me have her; they said she was unadoptable," he began explaining. "But I just couldn't leave her there. This may sound crazy—it seems crazy to me—but I think the reason I adopted her was that I knew nobody else would."

As we stood there looking down at that poor frightened little creature, I tried not to imagine what it must have been like for her inside a cage at the noisy, busy animal shelter.

Mr. Stanhope murmured, almost apologetically, "I call her Maizey because she's the color of creamed corn."

"You're not crazy, Mr. Stanhope," I said. "You're a man of action, that's all."

Now how was I going to get her out of there? Maizey had obviously taken one look at the enormous open expanse of the Stanhope kitchen and gone scurrying for the dimness of the den and wiggled her way behind the file cabinet. She was wedged front end first all the way in to the wall, head twisted back, trying to see the latest danger.

Ordinarily I do not approve of forcing any cat to accept my touch and my ministrations, but little Maizey would have to be bathed for her health's sake. That acid urine on her skin was producing more stress than a bath ever would. The way she had wedged herself back in there, I couldn't use any of my usual "Introduction of Self to New Cat" rituals. I couldn't extend my index finger slowly below chin level for her to sniff because of the way her head was twisted. The only approach was from above and that would seem threatening to her. As for extending my face to invite a nose touch, there was positively no way I could squeeze myself back there. So I opted for speed and efficiency: soonest done, soonest over, and, just like the man with the big leather gloves, I grabbed her by the scruff with one hand, slipped the other under her rump, lifted her up and whisked her out and onto the drainboard in the kitchen.

If you're afraid of a cat struggling or lashing out, just keep the cat moving. They'll usually stay quiet because they're off balance. The minute Maizey felt that drainboard under her feet, her reaction was like an explosion in all directions, screaming and lashing out with everything she had. My reflexes being what they are, no harm was done. I simply maintained a firm but gentle hold until she lay still. Whereupon she lost control of her bladder again and urinated onto the drainboard and down into the sink. Then, seeing no hope of escape, none at all, she slowly collapsed onto her side and lay there panting, awaiting the executioner's blade.

The bath was something of an anticlimax after that. I made it as quick and gentle as I could; Frederick was a dedicated assistant. I encouraged him to talk, to keep him as relaxed as possible, and so learned about his work, his apartment, and how he and Maizey had ended up together.

The warm dryer seemed to relax her a bit and as I worked I told Frederick how to make a Snug Retreat for her. When a cat is frightened and wants to hide, by all means, let her hide. But for convenience's sake, arrange a place you can easily get to, because you will want to give her eye and voice contact and food.

We settled her in the den closet behind the galoshes. She lay on a clean towel in a wine carton turned on its side. This simple setup was Maizey's own Snug Retreat. Frederick, his shirt front damp and wrinkled now, supplied a little bowl of water and a saucer of paté before we retired to the very inviting group of chairs on the other side of the room to discuss a plan of action.

"She's crippled inside, isn't she?" Mr. Stanhope said softly as he slumped into a chair. He seemed to feel he had bitten off more than he could chew.

"She's evidently suffered some bad emotional damage in the past," I began and stifled a yawn. I suddenly felt as if I was being enveloped by gray and tan, soft suede and muted teakwood. I became acutely aware of how incredibly tired I was. I tried to say something reassuring. "I've seen this sort of thing before. It's nothing that time and patience can't cure."

He gave me a doubtful look, reached for the crystal decanter on the big coffee table, and poured two glasses of sherry.

I breathed deeply, trying to dispel my sleepiness.

I hated to have to ask the next question: "Did you know that she has no front claws? She's been declawed."

"Has she, by heaven," he whispered, handing me a glass. "I'd no idea, no idea at all. I suppose that would explain a good deal, wouldn't it."

"Yes, it certainly would," I agreed. "But there are probably other reasons as well."

The absence of claws had become apparent during her outburst on the counter. I'm always extra polite and cautious when I work on a declawed cat. They're usually more nervous and defensive than a normal cat.

"But don't despair," I reassured him, "I've seen

many cats like this make a beautiful recovery. Of course, it can be a very long, slow process. Now, if you're game for that, I'll be glad to give you all the help I can."

Mr. Stanhope didn't hesitate. He was leaning forward, elbows on his knees. "What do we do first?" he asked.

When dealing with a troubled cat like Maizey, I always approach the problem from several angles at once: super nutrition, stress reduction, establishing new behavior patterns, and checking out the physical health. Since the ASPCA had declared her health to be "normal," I advised that we defer until a later date her visit to our own veterinarian. No veterinarian can do much of an exam on a hysterical cat with a racing heart anyway.

Not knowing what she had been fed previously, the goal of my dietary changes was twofold: building up health, while detoxifying her body and getting rid of old poisons and wastes.

Mr. Stanhope assured me that my homemade diet (see Basic Diet III, Appendix A) would present no problems to him at all. "Whatever is the best thing," he kept saying and nodded encouragement for me to go on.

The homemade food would be fresher, I explained, and so, easier for her to assimilate. Also, since the food was homemade we could be sure there would be no preservatives, colorings, chemical additives or sugar to irritate the nerves. These additives usually constitute a stress; they tend to increase tension and can cause hyperactivity in cats (as recent studies have shown to be the case with some children). To help

Maizey's mind deal with all the newness, plus her bad memories, I recommended giving her the Bach flower formula Rescue Remedy and also adding the anti-stress supplements (see Appendix A) to every meal.

Because of Maizey's hypersensitivity and extreme tension, I had to assume that she had previously been fed foods containing at least some chemicals and non-food additives. We would help her body to slowly eliminate these poisons by using a version of the Detoxification Program (see Appendix A).

To further reduce stress, I advised total permissiveness and a restricted area. Mr. Stanhope's apartment was large. Too much new territory all at once will confuse any cat and make her tense. New territory must be slowly explored, hiding places located, and potential dangers spotted and avoided. Mr. Stanhope would confine Maizey to a three-room area: the bathroom where her litter box was kept, the kitchen where her food and water would be, and the adjoining den where he always spent a good deal of his time. Now Maizey could get used to this little area at her own pace and begin to learn that Frederick was her friend. At Mr. Stanhope's suggestion, we set up another Snug Retreat in the kitchen closet and left the door ajar.

Establishing new patterns would consist of Mr. Stanhope signaling in advance every time he wanted to make contact with her. Giving a cat warning and then, even more important, allowing her to withdraw unhindered if she so chooses, are the quickest ways to give a frightened cat a feeling of security. Mr. Stanhope assured me he would remember to call her name, thereby announcing his presence, before entering a room. He would spend as many days as necessary on eye and voice contact, without insisting that she accept his touch. Then when she demonstrated her readiness for physical contact by leaning or moving toward him, he would present his hand slowly and below nose level for sniffing before he touched her.

"Remember," I told him, "familiarity breeds contentment for a pussycat. Cats feel secure in predictable circumstances. You can make her environment wonderfully predictable if you can manage to choreograph all your motions right before you do anything that involves her. Try to do everything exactly the same way each time and use the same words as well. Before long she'll begin to relax, you'll see. Just don't rush her."

"That's fine," he nodded slowly, "whatever she wants."

I left with my usual admonition to be sure to call me if he had any questions.

The first phone call wasn't long in coming—a day-and-a-half to be exact.

"She's not eating" was the gist of it.

"Has she eaten anything at all, even one lick?" I asked.

"Nothing since the paté, Miss Anitra. She's skipped three meals now."

"She ate the paté," I said, thinking aloud. "At least that was a starting point. What was in the paté?"

"Fish. You said don't give her any fish, so I couldn't let her have any more of that. It was Scotch salmon and whitefish with a little beluga caviar and some egg yolk, *crème fraîche*, and a few herbs."

Good grief, I hadn't realized it was a fish paté. "No," I said, "no, no, we don't want her to have that!"

My feeding instructions always caution against fish because the insoluble mineral salts it contains can cause bladder stones and gravel.

Mr. Stanhope explained that, patiently determined, he had made up several different meat, vegetable, and grain combinations each day—all to no avail. (See Diet, Appendix A.) What was the answer?

"Could you possibly be overcooking the chicken or meat?" I asked. "Cats prefer their meat rare."

There followed about four beats of dead silence.

"Mr. Stanhope, are you there?"

"Miss Anitra," came the quietly horrified response, "I am a chef of the Cordon Bleu."

Good grief, I should have guessed. I hastened to apologize. "Oh, Mr. Stanhope, I am terribly sorry. I had no idea."

"Quite all right, my dear." He seemed to have recovered. "No way you could have known."

I hastily switched the subject. "How does she seem otherwise? Is she using the litter? Is she drinking?"

"Well, yes, but she hasn't had a stool yet today." Mr. Stanhope was himself again. "She let me touch her this morning, but she just lies there looking so hopeless and lost and she's shedding to beat the band. I'm afraid she's going to lose all of her hair." Mr. Stanhope was worried. "Do you think she's getting sick?"

"Sounds like she's withdrawing. That's normal enough," I tried to reassure him. "But that excess shedding could mean she's detoxifying too fast. It would be best if we could get her to break her fast. Try mixing the paté half and half with the new food tonight, and let me know if she goes for it. Then if she's still not eating, we can try something else."

I would have to think the situation over and come up with a couple of contingency plans. I fervently hoped that it would not come down to force feeding. I've used that method—or finger feeding, as I prefer to call it—to help speed up the transition to new food, but with Maizey's fear of humans, I didn't like to even consider it. My thoughts turned quite naturally to a similar problem I was having at my place.

Problems always seem to come in bunches or pairs in my business, almost as if the Cat Goddess were sending you the first problem to prepare you so you'll be better able to solve it the second time around. Well, my first problem was a doozy and it wasn't entirely solved yet. In fact, he was sitting in my back playroom at that very moment. It occurred to me that it might be very reassuring for Mr. Stanhope to hear the story. Then he would know that Maizey wasn't the only cat who ever hid in a closet and refused food.

Timothy was an enormous gray male with green eyes. He was a middle-aged short-hair. Until he was ten, he had lived a private sort of life with a very nice lady in her fifties. The lady worked at home and Timothy was devoted to her.

Then the lady died of cancer. A friend of hers called me, very upset, to say that the police were about to "seal the apartment" and take Timothy away to the pound unless she could find somewhere to board him until she could place him in a new home. I usually don't do boarding, but, to make a long story short, I agreed to take him because of the unusual circumstances. She brought him over that evening, a sweet intelligent lady doing the only thing that was left to do for the friend she had lost.

"She would have done the same for me," she said. Timothy was growling and muttering inside the case. "He's turned quite wild ever since my friend left for the hospital the last time," she apologized. "It took all four of us to get him into the case."

"Four?"

"Three police officers and myself," she nodded. "He never was good with strangers, only with Mary . . . my friend. I don't know how I'm going to find anyone willing to take him."

The growling continued, *sotto voce,* inside the case. "Let's take this into the back room before we open it." I led the way. "It's quiet in here. I keep the 'spa' patients—the convalescent cats—in this room. There are only two here now." I opened the door, "Hi, girls, I brought someone to see ya."

The shy little blue cream Persian over by the scratching post blinked a greeting and looked doubtfully at the vibrating case in my hand. I set it down, opened the lid, and began to make introductions. "That one's Natasha. She's recovering from abdominal surgery. She swallowed a plastic bag two days before her owner had to leave for Cuernavaca."

I looked around the room and spotted a white tail tip peeking out of the Snug Retreat on top of the cabinet. "Powder-Puff had a bad eye infection. She has to be medicated six times a day, so she's staying here at the spa 'til she's better. Her owner works. They're both lovely sweet cats."

Well, Timothy didn't think they were lovely sweet

cats. He came out of that case with a roar, then stood stock still in the middle of the floor, growling enthusiastic hatred at everything in sight: me, the cats, the furniture and even his benefactress.

I stared in dismay. It wasn't his attitude that worried me so much as his appearance. My newest acquisition was enormously obese and covered with huge flakes of greasy dandruff. His head seemed much too tiny for his gross body; it looked as if it should have been given to a much smaller animal. His legs were skinny and ended in enormous floppy paws, each with six toes. He looked like a gray watermelon propped up on stilts, stuck into big fuzzy boxing gloves. Timothy was grotesque. Who indeed would ever want a cat like that?

With a final glare of hatred, which sent demure little Natasha whisking behind her scratching post, Timothy gave a sullen hiss, whirled around, and went scooting into the closet. And there he stayed for four days. He didn't eat, and he'd always begin growling the minute I walked into the room. If I so much as came near the closet, he would scream like a banshee. Natasha and Powder Puff were scandalized. I knew he was probably shedding like crazy in there because of the stress he was under and because he was fasting, but all I could see of him were two burning green orbs glaring out at me from the depths of the Snug Retreat I had installed for him before he arrived.

I understood how he must be feeling. He had lost the only human he ever knew; he had lost his home; he had been stuffed into a box and plunked down in strange territory with strange cats and a strange human who offered him strange food. If familiarity breeds contentment, it was no wonder that poor Timothy was going insane from insecurity. There wasn't one single familiar thing left to him. Furthermore, any cat who has a close relationship with his owner, as Timothy had, is sure to feel the owner's tension, sadness, pain, and fear. Knowing that his owner had died of cancer, I could well imagine what the emotional content of Timothy's life had been for the last couple of years.

I put water and a small litter box right by the closet door. It soon became apparent that he was drinking water and using the litter box at night.

On the fifth day he came out. When I walked into the room, the growling began. But it wasn't coming from the closet. Timothy was over on the windowsill. He would have to run past me to get back to his closet. He crouched down, and the hiss became a growl and the growl began to crescendo to that ear-splitting scream of his.

Inappropriate anger in cats should be ignored. Don't tell the cat not to do it or try to explain anything. In fact, try not to react in any way; that only makes it worse. Instead, turn away and speak quietly to another cat. Then do some mundane action that shows you are carrying on business as usual. Thus you will be demonstrating that there is no reason for anger or fear. I waited for a break between yells, then I spoke politely and casually to Natasha. This is like throwing a cat an emotional curve. In order to hear my voice, he had to change the yells to a hiss. Next I went to the dresser on the opposite side of the room from Timothy, turned my back, demonstrating lack of concern, stooped, demonstrating a non-threatening attitude, and opened and closed the bottom drawer, demonstrating that I hadn't come in to look at him at all, but to pursue some business of my own. Then, without looking at Timothy again, I rose and strolled out of the room.

Timothy was back in the closet for the rest of the day, but for the next two days he kept sneaking out. He was preparing to consider that I just might be harmless. I kept demonstrating like crazy—opening and closing drawers, wiping off dresser tops, and doing a lot of petting and talking to Natasha and Powder Puff so he could witness how casual and relaxed we were with each other.

The fact that Timothy came out of the closet at all meant he definitely was going to be all right—eventually. If you avoid the trap of concerning yourself with speed of progress, then all will proceed at its own pace and you can simply create a permissive and stress-free environment, observe, and learn. Think of it in the same way as growing a flower: you can prepare the soil and you can water the seed, but you can't hurry the growth by pulling the flower upward. It's like that when you're re-patterning a difficult cat's personality traits.

As with Maizey, I had the additional problem of introducing the new food. Cat owners are not nutritionists, they are simply nice people who love their cats. And even if they do read labels, they often don't know the meaning of half the ingredients listed there (unless they've read the chapter, "What's Really in Pet Food" in the book *Dr. Pitcairn's Complete Guide to Natural Health for Dogs and Cats)*. And so they are easily influenced by skillful Madison Avenue advertising. Consequently, almost any cat that comes to me has been eating one or more of the three "no-nos"—

dry food, semi-moist food, or fish—as all or part of his previous diet.

Many cats are addicted to a single food. Veterinarians call such cats "tuna junkies" or "dry food junkies," or, since semi–moist foods are up to 15 percent sugar, cats who will only eat this are called "sugar junkies." Addicted cats believe that their food is the only existing edible substance. Anything else is just not food at all to them. Making a dietary changeover for such a cat is terribly difficult—but definitely possible and certainly necessary if you want to achieve normal health.

A cat can fast safely for five days. Several veterinarians have told me the same thing, and I know it's true because I have seen several cats fast for five days. But I do not recommend it. As a general rule, I prefer a gentler approach. I have frequently recommended fasting from one to three days to help a cat deal with a variety of different problems (see Fasting, Appendix A), one of which is easing a cat into a dietary change. But it must be remembered that, during a fast, the body cleans out a lot of old toxins built up from whatever harmful products the cat has eaten before. Preservatives, food colorings, and chemical additives are all stored in the body fat, and, as the fat melts away, these substances are released into the bloodstream to be processed out of the body by the kidneys, liver, and intestines. If these toxins are released too rapidly for the body to take care of, there will be a backup of wastes that can cause such problems as skin rash, runny nose, or other discharge. These symptoms are usually not serious. They are simply signs that the body is successfully cleaning itself out. They will pass shortly if left alone. But why not avoid these little annoyances if we can do so, simply by proceeding a bit more slowly.

So I don't worry if a cat, like Maizey, skips three meals. I just make very sure she is drinking and using the litter. If her kidneys are passing off wastes the way they should, the urine will smell strong. Then, after a three- or four-meal fast (refusal to eat *one morsel*), and having tried feeding three or four healthful combinations of homemade food, I always recommend partially giving in—but only partially. Now is when I advise owners to mix old food and the new diet half and half.

In the case of Maizey, the old food was fish. When a cat has fasted for three to four meals (one and a half or two days), she will be hungry, and, as they say, hunger is the best sauce. When you present the half-and-half mixture, the cat will probably eat. Then just keep decreasing the ratio of the old food and increasing the new.

There are a couple of warnings to heed, however. Warning number one is, don't give a normal-sized portion. There are three reasons for this. First, a hungry cat will eat quickly, and if he also eats a lot, he's sure to throw it up. Second, and most important, since you want to keep decreasing the amount of low-quality food you're mixing with the healthful new food, you must keep the appetite lively so the cat will continue to eat the food even though it tastes less and less like what he's been used to. Third, you must be able to see whether the cat has eaten *any* food at all. If you put a big mound of food on the plate, you won't be able to tell if he has taken a few licks or not, and that is *very* important. If the cat eats even one or two licks, you have overcome a very important facet of the problem, because this means that the cat has now decided that the food you are feeding him is edible. One teaspoonful morning and evening is a nice little snack for a cat. It's a good start. Remember, he is at least ten times smaller than you, so multiply the amount he eats by ten to get an idea of what a comparable amount would be for you. My own method is to serve one teaspoonful so I can see exactly how much the cat eats. If he cleans it up, I give another, and another, up to three or four—but no more at any meal, until we have reached the goal of eating only the high-quality foods with none of the old "no-nos."

Warning number two is, don't keep the food available after mealtime is over. Remove all food after a half-hour. Leave fresh water available all the time. Owners sometimes reason, "maybe he'll finish it if I leave it down for a while." In the first place, he probably won't, and in the second place, smelling the food for hours at a time will very surely ruin the very appetite you're trying to foster. In other words, you would be working against yourself. Instead, remove the food after a half-hour and at the next meal again feed only a teaspoonful. You can vary the menu slightly, changing the vegetable or trying lamb or liver instead of chicken or beef.

In the end you will win, because you have two unbeatable weapons on your side—perseverance and love. Love always wins.

Following my policy of total permissiveness, Timothy was permitted to eat in the closet at first. Later he decided that the windowsill was all right, and finally he joined the girls with his plate next to theirs on the newspaper on the floor. He was finally eating what they ate—my homemade diet.

When Timothy first came out of the closet, he would hiss on eye contact. That ceased after three days of my calmly ignoring it. When I walked in the following day, he simply stood up from his lounging spot on the windowsill and started pacing back and forth.

I could see he had lost a little weight, close to a half-pound, actually, but he was still a gray watermelon. He plopped back down on the windowsill and began trying, unsuccessfully, to groom his anal area. His stomach was still so big he couldn't reach beyond his knees; he just kept rolling over sideways and coming up against the window screen, boxing gloves alternately flailing in the air and scrabbling on the sill. Graceful, he wasn't.

The dandruff was definitely going away, though. I looked three times before I could believe that. Fasting makes improvements happen fast, so I shouldn't have been too surprised. His ruff area was beginning to fluff out a bit as well. I felt encouraged. Now with the new diet going full swing, he'd be back to normal in a couple of months—physically anyway. It's true that nerves are part of the physical body, and proper nutrition will do a lot toward calming and healing a nervous, troubled cat; but I knew that Timothy would need time, a lot more time, before he'd really relax and begin to enjoy life again.

I was scheduled to drop by the Stanhope apartment the following day. Frederick was beaming triumphantly as he opened the door.

"She's eating!" he announced, gleeful as a scientist who has found the secret formula. The army fatigues had been replaced by a navy blue jogging suit. He fairly bounded with enthusiasm as he led the way back to the kitchen.

"I'm using the paté formula, keeping the paté texture, but substituting chicken liver, chicken breast, potato, and egg. For flavoring I simply add a quarter teaspoon of beluga caviar," he finished with a flourish as we approached the kitchen closet. It was open just a crack.

"Maizey," he called softly, hand on the knob, "may we look in, dear?" He opened the door and the light fell all the way into the back of the closet. There was the unadoptable cat curled up on the thick bath towel inside the wine crate behind Frederick's galoshes. She didn't look too good. Her fur was lank and thin. The towel on the bottom of the box was covered with large clumps of yellow hair. Her eyes were wide with alarm, but she wasn't trembling.

I blinked a greeting to her. She blinked back automatically before she remembered to be frightened. Then, confused, she skittered around the side of her box and tried to burrow in behind it.

"Does she come out at all?" I asked.

"Oh, yes." He stooped down, crooning, "Today we even sat at the door of the den and watched Daddy for quite a while, didn't we, Maizey?" Mr. Stanhope turned to me. "Doesn't her fur look better?"

Actually, I didn't think so, but then I couldn't see it very well. It certainly didn't look any worse. So I just said, "It looks like she's been cleaning herself. Has she?"

"Why, yes. Is that a good sign?"

"It's a very good sign," I said. "It means she's relaxing a bit. I don't like all that shedding, though. I think we'd better get a few vegetables and some extra lecithin into your paté."

Before I left I made a few suggestions for Maizey's paté. Chicken liver, chicken breast, and potato was certainly a very good beginning, but it lacked bulk to help the wastes pass through the intestine. Maizey's oily coat showed that her body was having difficulty disposing of wastes. The formula lacked minerals, vitamins, and bulk. Over the next two weeks Mr. Stanhope would begin adding pureed vegetables, lightly steamed or raw, and the Vita-Mineral Mix (see Appendix A).

I also suggested trying to find a crunchy treat she would enjoy; that's always a good way to add variety to the menu. Mr. Stanhope took down the whole list of acceptable treats (see Appendix A), determined to try them all.

"And how is little Timothy?" he asked as we walked to the door.

"He's progressing nicely, thank you," I said laughing, "but 'little Timothy' is still absolutely enormous, I'm afraid."

"Oh, yes," Mr. Stanhope smiled, "I forgot. He has a weight problem. But how are his spirits, poor little chap?"

To kindly Mr. Stanhope, lonely Timothy was a "poor little chap." I pictured the huge gray watermelon snarling at me from the windowsill.

"He needs quite a bit more time, I think—just like Maizey. He's trying to learn to trust, but he just can't seem to bring himself to relax. He hasn't formed any relationships yet."

Mr. Stanhope shook his head sadly. "Poor little chap. Give him our regards, won't you. We're rooting for him, you know."

Over the next three weeks, Timothy progressed to the point where he would accept food from my hand. Twice I "accidentally" brushed against his fur and we both pretended to ignore the mistake. Definite progress—small, but definite.

His lady benefactor continued to pay for his board and apologized for not finding someone to take him off my hands.

"It's perfectly all right," I assured her. "He presents an interesting personality problem, poor little chap." I was beginning to sound like Mr. Stanhope.

I saw Maizey every week for a while, mainly to keep an eye on her health. I combed her a little on my fourth visit. She was a great deal calmer now. She had settled in, and Frederick, the intrepid chef, had found a way to get her to eat every nutrient I had suggested. As for the crunchy treats, Frederick concocted some perfectly delightful little whole wheat croutons with a buttery garlic aroma that would drive any cat wild with desire.

The coat is a barometer of the cat's health, so it was gratifying to see Maizey's coat begin to fluff out a bit after her diet was broadened. She was still too quiet, though, far too timid, and she had grown completely dependent upon Frederick.

"She has to be able to see me at all times," he said with a worried frown. "I have to fly to London next month, and I don't know what I'm going to do. I hate to leave her even for a few hours as it is."

I think it was at that moment that the germ of an idea began to sprout in my mind. I needed time to think it over. "I'll give it some thought," I said. "Don't worry, we'll work something out."

Maizey was lucky. Frederick was the perfect owner for a cat like that. He had all the necessary qualities for dealing with an emotionally damaged cat: patience, love, and willingness to learn. He was just the sort of owner I needed to find for Timothy. And Maizey could be just what Timothy needed because, besides a totally permissive environment, cats also need some purpose in life—some sort of responsibility to give them direction and self-esteem.

Maizey needed a companion for when Frederick went out, but it had to be a cat's cat who would focus on her and not compete with her for Frederick's attention. Whatever Timothy had been in the past, he was now a cat's cat. I wondered . . .

Timothy's shape began to approach that of a normal cat. The body and head looked as if they belonged together at last. He was still overweight, but at least he could reach all the parts of his body to wash himself. His coat took on a plushy quality and I was dying to touch it—but he didn't enjoy it, so I restrained the impulse. Natasha and Powder Puff had both recuperated fully and returned to their respective homes. They had looked upon Timothy with disdain after all that screaming. They had never even begun to get close to him. It was their choice; they were both very staid and reserved ladies. His present roommate, MacDuff, was seventeen years old and suffering from a heart condition. Timothy often sat next to him, even lay against him, sharing body warmth, but that was the extent of their socializing. The old boy slept most of the time.

Timothy ate the large servings of high-quality food I mixed with bran and water. He was well on the way to becoming a very fine figure of a cat—physically. What he lacked was a relationship. Timothy needed a friend.

"Shall we tell Auntie Anitra what we did this morning?" Frederick enjoyed the grooming sessions as much as Maizey. Prokofiev's "Romeo and Juliet Suite" was playing softly in the den. I caught a glimpse of warm color through the open door; I looked again and saw a row of plum and forest green cushions strewn across the gray couch. Maizey was lounging on the marble counter top opposite the sink. I was in the process of "finger grooming" her—a technique of mine which acclimates the cat to being touched all over before I use a tool. It's really a massage which gives me a chance to explore the coat and body. The cats always enjoy it so I like to keep it in the routine, even for very relaxed old clients. Maizey had learned to trust me and even to enjoy this part of her beauty treatment. The high-quality diet was strengthening her nerves as well as her body.

"And what was it my Princess did this morning?" I asked her.

Frederick became serious. "Anitra, I'm afraid she's going to fall into the tub. She just won't leave me alone. When I take my bath in the morning, she keeps trying to get to me by walking across the bubbles. I've had to catch her twice or she would have gone tumbling in."

"Oh, Maizey!" I exclaimed. "You didn't do that, did you?"

I lifted Maizey down from the counter and our refugee from the animal shelter favored us with a promenade once around the kitchen, tail held high, then disappeared into the den.

"She's becoming quite a beauty," I smiled.

"And well she knows it," Frederick agreed, watching her go.

"Oh, by the way," I remarked casually, gathering up the grooming tools, "Timothy sends you his regards . . . poor little chap."

Frederick was immediately serious again. "How is he progressing?"

"Well, wonderfully, actually . . . as far as his body is concerned anyway. He's developing into an impressive big cat. He's strong as an ox, healthy as a horse . . . physically anyway." I began washing the tools in the sink.

"Only physically?" Frederick prompted.

"He's lonely." I sighed and shook my head. "He loved one owner for ten years, then she died. He's too much in shock to be able to form a relationship with another human. And all the cats he's met are either too sick or too snooty to give him the time of day. He is desperately alone." I looked Frederick square in the eye. "And no one will ever want him. He has been too badly damaged emotionally, and, well, to be frank, Frederick, if I were to attempt to describe Timothy's physical attributes, the words 'sinuous grace' would not exactly spring to my lips."

"I know. I know. His weight problem, you mean."

I shook my head. "No. His weight is almost normal now. It's his feet I'm talking about."

"His feet?" Frederick was becoming intrigued.

"Frederick, did you know that all through history six-toed cats have been considered to be very lucky?"

"He has six toes?!"

"On every foot, I'm afraid. He looks like he's walking on boxing gloves. Timothy is what I would call an interesting cat. Maizey is beautiful . . . Timothy is interesting." I went back to busily drying my tools. "But few people can appreciate a cat like that. No one will ever want him, poor little chap."

"Poor little chap," Frederick echoed. "All alone."

"Just like Maizey was when you got her," I interjected.

"Just like . . ." Then he caught on. "Anitra! Do you mean . . . do you think I should try Timothy as a friend for Maizey? Do you think they might like each other?"

"Frederick, do you remember that first night when you told me you wanted a cat to provide interest and liven this place up? Well, I'd be willing to bet that Timothy is that cat."

"Well," Frederick raised his hands. "None of that matters really, Anitra. If Maizey and he like each other, that's all I care about."

Bless the man!

Frederick's gaze wandered about the den. "It is a happy coincidence though, isn't it? His being gray, I mean."

A proper introduction would go a long way toward ensuring a smooth beginning for the relationship. The person introducing the two cats should be a stranger to both, so my assistant Valerie would perform the introduction, as she had so many times in the past.

Frederick set Maizey up beautifully beforehand by giving her so much physical affection and attention he practically made a pest of himself. When Valerie brought Timothy into that abode of tranquility that Frederick had designed, Maizey was one very secure pussycat. There was no doubt in her mind that she was loved.

When doing introductions, we always include the twelve basic steps given in Carole C. Wilbourn's book, *The Inner Cat*. The object of the introduction ritual is to demonstrate to the old cat that the new cat is no threat to her security—he is not replacing her in the owner's heart. I explained to Frederick that he must behave as if he had no interest whatsoever in this new cat. "You must act in every way as if the newcomer belongs to Valerie, the person who brought him in, and has nothing to do with you, and you must continue to ignore him for several days until Maizey accepts him and brings him to you. Since you cannot explain this in words, you must demonstrate the fact by your actions."

Having a stranger bring in the new cat associates the newcomer with the stranger in your cat's mind. If the stranger then sits and chats a while, holding the new cat in a carrier on her lap, the association will be further strengthened. A good rule to go by is this: the slower the introduction proceeds, the quieter and less stressful it will be.

I warned Frederick that Valerie would ask him to stay away from the cats as much as possible for the first hour or so. If the owner and the stranger must stay in the same room as the cats, they should keep talking about unrelated matters and not focus on the interaction of the cats.

Remember, the slower it goes, the better, so if the two felines just sit and stare at each other for what seems like an interminable length of time, that's great! The two humans can then consider going out for coffee, as Valerie and Frederick did. This will demonstrate to the cats that any thought of crisis or trouble is the farthest thing from your mind.

I warned Frederick that hissing is normal. The humans should ignore it. It is a signal, among cats, that the introduction must proceed slower still. It is simply a cat's way of saying, "Stay away, I'm not ready to let you come closer yet."

If any real threats are made, such as actual screaming, one can provide a distraction without letting the cats know that the distraction has anything to do with them. For example, suddenly turn the radio or television up very loud and then down again or walk into the kitchen and just happen to drop a pan and lid onto the floor. In a dire emergency, if fur is flying, you can break up a fight by spraying water into both cats' faces or you can simply lower a large cardboard box over one cat, until you can get the other one out of the room. Things very seldom come to such a pass. The finale of the introduction is leaving the cats alone together.

Valerie, giving me the story later on, said that Maizey ran from her, and Timothy ran from Frederick, so the two cats were left in their separate hiding places and the humans went into the living room for a glass of wine.

They returned a half-hour later to find Maizey perched up on one kitchen chair and Timothy crouched under another only two feet away. The two cats were having eye contact, but when Valerie and Frederick came in, Timothy bolted into the den and Maizey followed. After five minutes passed with no sounds of distress or combat from the den, Valerie announced that the introduction could be safely left in the hands of the cats. She told me later that she thought Frederick was "a nice owner," which, from Valerie, is the highest accolade.

By the time I saw Maizey for her next weekly grooming, an attachment had been formed. Timothy had transferred his old owner devotion to Maizey, the most fascinating cat he had ever known. I must admit, I had to agree with Timothy. The former "unadoptable cat" had turned into quite a looker, with her shiny creamed corn coat and dainty little shell pink ears and a nose to match. Maizey carried herself like a cat who knew she was a queen.

"She bullies him unmercifully," Frederick beamed at the couple, "and he just dotes on her." He reached down and began stroking Maizey under the chin. "I'm seeing a whole new side of my girl now that she has a gentleman admirer. Anitra, I left them alone all day Thursday, and when I got home, she came to meet me and gave me a scolding for being gone so long, but she was fine. Timothy is always right behind her, you know; he follows her like a shadow. I think he's happy here too."

Indeed, I could see that he was, standing there straight and tall on those boxing glove feet. Timothy, gazing fondly at Maizey, was a cat who had found his place in the world—he was a cat with responsibility, a cat with a relationship. As for Maizey, what else could she do but blossom and bloom in the midst of all that love.

I was feeling jocular. "I think they compliment the decor nicely, don't you, Frederick? Gray and tan . . ."

"Good gracious, no," he replied, throwing up his hands in mock alarm. "We're doing the whole place over. Maizey herself has chosen the dominant color, didn't you, darling."

He began rummaging in a small pile of pamphlets on the counter, found the one he was looking for, and spread it out. It was a folder of paint color samples in the pink family, ranging from light to dark.

"This is it," he announced, pointing to one, a tastefully subdued tannish pink. "This is the one she chose. Timothy quite agrees with her and so do I." He looked up expectantly. "You recognize the color, of course."

I took a closer look. Under the color square was printed, "Number 14." No clue there. I looked back at Frederick, who prompted quietly, "It's Cat's Nose Rose."

"Cat's Nose Rose," I hooted, and then we were all laughing fit to bust.

CLAWED'S STORY

CHAPTER FIVE

CLAWED'S STORY
The Older Cat

I'VE ALWAYS been a great one for adopting elderly cats. Most people want kittens, but I guess I just got an overdose of that great American urge to fight for the underdog—or the undercat, as the case may be.

Over the past twelve years my apartment has been host to dozens of "undercats" of the geriatric variety, lounging about, enjoying their sunset days. The cats all came burdened with particular physical ailments and have paid their bills by giving me new knowledge as I tried to solve their problems.

Old Clawed Quincy was the cat who taught me the most. He was my very first geriatric cat. Coming from a background of neglect, as he did, he was a regular walking textbook of elderly cat ailments. Also, because of him, I was faced for the first time with a delicate moral dilemma that I had, up to that point in my relatively new career, managed to avoid.

Clawed lived the first fifteen years of his life with

the Quincys, a wealthy and intellectual family of four. He had once been cherished, been loved and fondled, but that was many years ago. The children were young then, and Clawed had arrived as a tiny white fluff ball curled up inside a shoebox under the Christmas tree. As far as I could piece the story together, there had followed many happy years of adventure and fun. Clawed slept night after blissful night curled close beside a youngster's ear, and in the mornings there was always romping under the sheets.

Childhood diseases came and went, and Clawed rose to these occasions with soothing purrs and gentle washings with a tongue that scratched and tickled young wrists and fingers. Obviously Clawed felt deeply his responsibility to his human family.

A real pedigreed Persian, Clawed was the pride of the household. He had long, snow-white fur and huge copper eyes that sparkled like new pennies most of the time. But that, as I say, was many years ago.

Now the children were grown and had gone away to school, the parents were immersed in their own careers, and Clawed had become a sort of retired cat. No one had paid him much attention for the past few years until, this winter, it was discovered that copious amounts of dandruff had appeared in his fur and were being shed all over the furniture and the rugs. The busy Quincys had neither the time nor the patience to clean up after a cat who was no longer a vital member of the household, and so, at this point, just before Clawed's fifteenth Christmas, I was called in to "give him a bath or something!"

Mr. Quincy, tall and distinguished, greeted me at the door and, after doffing my overcoat and boots, I was led in to the exquisitely appointed living room, where an equally exquisite Mrs. Quincy smiled, grasped my hand, and gestured in the direction of the sofa.

"And this is Clawed," she caroled gaily.

At the sound of her voice, a dull white mound under the end table began to stir and unfold and a sad little face peeked diffidently out at me.

"Clawed's been a naughty boy, getting dandruff and hair all over the apartment," she cooed, wagging her finger in Clawed's direction. "Miss Anitra's going to get you all nice and clean now, Clawed."

The uppermost thought in my mind was that dandruff was probably the least of Clawed's problems. To begin with, those big copper eyes were exuding a nasty brown discharge, and, as the cat began wobbling unsteadily to his feet, I could see that his front legs were slightly deformed. His ankles buckled badly inward with his weight back on his heels. The toes, I observed, were flopping softly out to each side. As he stood there, swaying ever so gently, a look of polite inquiry on his face, he reminded me of nothing so much as an elderly ballet master with fallen arches. Clawed was definitely not a well cat.

I picked the old boy up and carried him very gently out to the kitchen counter. Bones were all I could feel, no muscle tone, no firm flesh. Then, as I began stroking my fingers through the sparse hair, examining the oily skin, Clawed gave a yawn and stretched himself out full length on the counter; he trusted me. I hadn't combed him more than three strokes when a magnificent purr came rumbling out of that bedraggled old body to fill the Quincy's shiny kitchen with the sound of a cat's contentment. Clawed was obviously hungry for affection.

Old Clawed relaxed into those warm suds like a tired executive. When I began the deep massage he looked up, gave me a long blissful blink, and lowered his purr to a murmur. Mr. and Mrs. Quincy were enjoying the whole scene to the hilt, so I decided to seize the opportunity and ask a few pertinent questions about their cat's sorry state.

That was when I was told about Clawed's "retired status," which explained his depressed attitude. I also discovered that the diet they were providing consisted mainly of one of those dry foods that are supposed to be so wonderful because they are "low in ash." The Quincys served it in one of those automatic dispensers which was left available twenty-four hours a day. So, I had an explanation for the dandruff as well. In former days, it seems, when the kids were in charge of Clawed's menu, their idea of a high-class diet for a high-class cat had been nothing but sliced roast beef and turkey. This is a terrific beginning, but hardly what one could call balanced nutrition, since there was no roughage, no bulk. He would probably be suffering from constipation. Since there was very little calcium in sliced meats he would probably have porous bones as well, hence the buckling ankles. To top it all off, his kidneys would probably be exhausted from the protein imbalance. Failing kidneys is a sure cause of dandruff. And, incidentally, Clawed hadn't seen the inside of a veterinarian's office in nigh on to seven years.

I pointed out to the Quincys that Clawed missed their attention. To illustrate this I asked Mrs. Quincy to hold his head and stroke his throat during the blow drying. Old Clawed was floating on Cloud Nine. His eyes were squinting in an ecstasy of sensual pleasure and he was making crooked little ineffectual kneading motions with his feet on the towel. He obviously adored the lady.

When I broached the subject of a higher quality diet, I encountered a blank wall. Feline nutrition was definitely not within the Quincys' realm of interest. I gently pointed out that Clawed's vaccination was long overdue, and I was relieved when they said, "Well, he might as well have one, and get a thorough examination at the same time."

"We'd rather pay for the veterinarian than spend a lot of time fussing with food," Mrs. Quincy explained. "It's easier." Obviously what was "easier" for Clawed hadn't entered their minds. Before I left, I myself made an appointment for Clawed to see Dr. McAlister the very next day. I was hoping that, if the facts were presented by a veterinarian, then the Quincys might finally agree that some major dietary and lifestyle changes should be made.

I made sure that they had my telephone number and I suggested they call me after they saw the doctor, because then I could design a diet based on her diagnosis and we could help Old Clawed get back at least some of his former health and beauty. I was finding Old Clawed irresistible, and I just could not imagine how anybody else wouldn't feel exactly the same way.

Two days went by and I didn't hear from the Quincys. I thought about Clawed, sweet Old Clawed sitting proudly atop the hassock after his blow drying, a new cat. Without a change of diet and at least a little bit of T.L.C., Clawed would very rapidly revert to being a very old cat again.

"Forget Clawed," I told myself. "A lack of professional detachment leads to emotional exhaustion." I used to collect truisms my first few years on the job. I soon learned, however, that they are easier said than done, and, as Day Two drew to a close, I had decided that professional detachment need not necessarily prohibit a tiny bit of professional curiosity. So I put in a call to the veterinarian's office and had the receptionist pull out Clawed's card and read me the data entered by Dr. McAlister. Clawed had been found to be about 85 percent deaf, a common enough state of affairs in old cats who have been on a poor diet. It was nothing to get too excited about. However, he was also arthritic in his lower spine and both hip joints. He had been found to have severe rickets in all four legs and, to top it all off, just as I feared, his kidneys were all shriveled up, with very little function left.

Clawed's body was breaking down, but none of these conditions were irreversible. Arthritic deposits in and around the joints can slowly be dissolved. Kidney tissue can be healed and slowly regenerate. Weak and porous bones can be recalcified and strengthened again. Clawed could still look forward to several years of quiet pleasure, warm and secure in the midst of the family he loved.

A total of four days dragged by and Clawed's owners still hadn't called me. The pre-Christmas rush of bathing requests had me zooming all over town on my bike. The temperature was hovering up in the forties and I hoped it would hold. In spare moments at home

I kept my mind directed toward positive pursuits, cro-
cheting the woolen mouse toys that I was giving as
Christmas presents that year. But, try as I might, I
could not get Old Clawed out of my mind.

"Worrying over something about which you can do
nothing is a shameful waste of energy," I reminded
myself. But still my thoughts kept running back to Old
Clawed and the Quincys.

"Maybe they forgot," I told myself. "Maybe they
didn't want to bother me. Maybe they lost my number." I gave in and called them about an hour after
dinner on the fourth day.

Mr. Quincy answered and said right away that they
had just been talking about calling me. I breathed a
sigh of relief, but I wasn't relieved for long. Clawed's
condition had gotten worse. The dandruff was back as
bad as ever and all he did, said Mr. Quincy, was sleep,
drink the water dish dry and run to the litter box.

I began to explain to Mr. Quincy that these were
all symptoms of failing kidneys, which would improve
to a surprising extent as soon as we got his diet in hand,
but he cut me short and then began to beat about the
bush. First he told me how they'd always wanted the
best for Old Clawed; then about how busy they both
were and how lonely it must be for Old Clawed now
that the children were gone; and how a cat couldn't
be happy anyway with all that messy dandruff all over
his skin. And then, finally, he came to the point. Mr.
Quincy wanted to know if I would be so kind as to
come over, pick up Clawed, and "drop him off" at the
veterinarian's office to be put to sleep.

So, there it was. Sometimes I argue for the cat and
sometimes, when I sense that it won't do any good

anyway, I don't. This was, I think, my first experience with an owner whose mind was firmly closed. The Quincys had obviously concocted some pretty fancy rationalizations to support this decision; the last thing they wanted now was to listen to facts.

The sort of commitment in time and effort that Clawed needed now was not what the Quincys had bargained for fifteen years ago when they bought their children a little white fluff ball. They hadn't thought about it then and they didn't want to think about it now.

I didn't want to think about it either. My mind was in a state of semi-shock. I wanted to hang up because I needed a few moments to handle what was happening. So I told Mr. Quincy I'd be over right away.

I took a taxi. The temperature was dropping. Crossing Eighty-sixth Street, I watched the Christmas shoppers leaning into the wind, blinking away the snowflakes swirling into their faces, and tried to prepare my mind for what I had to do next.

"At least," I told myself, "Clawed won't be left alone to die slowly of neglect and loneliness." Clawed, who purred when you touched him. I quickly turned my thoughts away from the purring and concentrated on the snow and the frost forming on the cab window.

When I arrived at the Quincys, I found that they seemed to want to get the thing over as quickly as possible, for when Mr. Quincy opened the door he had the carrier in hand with Clawed huddled dismally inside. As he handed the case over to me, there was no sound from Clawed. He was just a weight, a weight that was much too light, transferred into my hands.

Mr. Quincy tried to speak, failed, and then said, much too loudly, "How much do you . . . how much should . . . how much is it?"

The emotions I saw on his face were many. But under it all I saw guilt, guilt that he couldn't face and would never admit to. And I knew very clearly, in the same moment that I accepted that old cat's weight, that this man would have to live with that guilt for the rest of his life. Poor man, if he ever did come to an understanding, it would be too late.

I retreated into my businesslike manner. "I'll take care of everything," I said. "I'll hold Clawed when he's put to sleep so that he won't be with strangers. Dr. McAlister can bill you for the injection and cremation. As far as my fee is concerned, I work by the hour. My fee is the same as it was for grooming." It was a relief when the door closed.

Down in the lobby the kindly doorman suggested I have a seat while he went out to look for a cab. Snow flew like ash around the doorman's black umbrella. As I sat there hugging Clawed's carrier and watching the big white flakes settle and melt, settle and melt, certain moral questions began breaking through into my conscious mind, clamoring to be resolved.

I had performed this service before, but always it had been for clients I knew well and only after long and careful consultation with the doctor. It had always been after we knew for certain that life was unpleasant for our friend and that we had no hope of bringing him comfort again. If Clawed was not in pain, if he was still capable of enjoying such pleasures as the bath and blow drying and petting and massage and attention and food, was it then morally correct to put him to death?

On the other hand, his owners were not prepared to give him any of these pleasures. Clawed was not my cat, and I had given my word to his owners that I would carry out their wish.

Fate had brought Clawed and me together. At least now there was a loving and responsible person in charge, I told myself, someone who could make sure that Clawed would be secure and comfortable and relaxed all the way through to the end.

I knew perfectly well that every day thousands of young, healthy cats are routinely destroyed by animal shelters simply because there is no room for them. It was highly unprofessional, I chided myself, to become emotionally upset over one sick old specimen simply because he and I had become briefly acquainted. Years before I had wrestled with the question of taking a life—something which can't be given back—and had finally come to the conclusion that terminal suffering should be cut short. But was Clawed suffering? And even if he were, was it actually terminal, or could a caring person give him a few extra days, or weeks, or months of quiet pleasure? And then there I was, back at square one—the owners were not willing to do it. My professional detachment lay in tatters at my feet by the time the doorman was back to announce the arrival of my taxi.

As I seated myself inside and started to tell the driver my destination, the crowning blunder of the evening dawned on me: Dr. McAlister's office was long closed for the night, and here I was with a sick old cat in my lap. There was only one thing left to do; I would just have to take Clawed home with me until tomorrow.

"Until tomorrow" ... what a laugh. Clawed was destined to spend a contented four *years* with me. In the end, the moral quandry had boiled down to only one thing: Was Clawed in pain?

The next day, after Dr. McAlister had finished a thorough geriatric workup, I asked her straight out. "Is Clawed in any pain?"

"Pain, no." She gently palpated his lower back above the hip socket. "His kidneys are not causing pain. He will have an occasional twinge of arthritis, of course, and there is a nasty gum infection caused by that filthy tartar, but overall he is simply tired. The kidney disease, the bone porosity, these things are serious of course, but they're not giving him any actual pain. He's just old, Anitra. Do you understand what I mean? He's just terribly old."

He was also terribly loving, and terribly outgoing, and warm, and responsive, and purring like a buzz saw lounging there on that metal examining table.

I had made up my mind to a course of action, and I had a strong hunch that Dr. McAlister would probably go along with me on it. "Okay," I said, "just suppose I were to take him home for a while, and give him a nice quiet place and supply him with all the nutrients his body needs, to repair the kidneys and strengthen the bones."

Dr. McAlister was shifting into her lecturing pose, so I grabbed a quick breath and hurried on. "I know I promised the Quincys I'd put him to sleep, but I never said *when* I'd do it. Well, just look at him." I gestured to Clawed who was, thank the Cat Goddess, blinking trustfully up at Dr. McAlister and still purring in his most resonant tones.

Dr. McAlister sighed and shook her head, but she didn't say no, so I pressed my advantage.

"Now I know you can't clean his teeth because his kidneys aren't strong enough to stand the anesthetic. But suppose you were to clean just one tooth, one a month. Then you wouldn't need anesthesia. I'll bring him in once a month and you can scale one or two teeth and you can check his progress at the same time. You and I will keep a close watch on him, and whenever you tell me that things are getting too uncomfortable for him, well, then we can put him to sleep."

Dr. McAlister was opening Clawed's mouth again, muttering "filthy, just filthy," as she carefully worked the tooth scaler in between a chunk of greyish yellow tartar and the gum line. Then, with a firm downward pressure, she dislodged the piece onto her waiting index finger and flung it into the metal tray. Success! But before I could press my advantage further, she held up her hand. "All right, Anitra, all right. I suppose you can give it a try if you want to."

"I want to," I said.

So Clawed was mine now, and I had to admit that that was really the way I'd wanted it from the start.

The night before, when Clawed and I had shown up back at the apartment, Purr, Florence, and Priscilla had made no objections to the sudden addition of a house guest. This was probably because the bewildered cat I lifted out of the carry case was at such a low energy level that even my imaginative Florence couldn't pretend that he posed any sort of a threat to her position as reigning queen of the household. In fact, introducing a new cat to the household turned out to be no problem at all. For this I was grateful, since by that time I was feeling just about as tired as Clawed looked.

As soon as I lifted Clawed out onto the floor, he spotted my little keyhole desk up against the radiator and made straight for that. He padded into the opening, circled once around, the tips of his fur brushing the hot radiator and, unable to bend his legs sufficiently to achieve a graceful landing, collapsed with a plop onto the floor. His eyes were full of confusion and sadness, and he didn't look as if he could get up enough spirit to take a drink of water.

Big Purr, who was still young enough to be thrilled, glided over to investigate Clawed's extended hind foot. He stopped, nose suspended about one millimeter from the upturned pad, and sniffed appreciatively.

Clawed didn't respond. His chin rested softly on the big floppy paws, his eyes staring at nothing in particular. Clawed was in mourning. For fifteen years he had loved the Quincys. He loved them now, as always, and he seemed to sense somehow that he was not going to see them again, not ever. He didn't know any of the "whys"—but why didn't matter to Clawed. Nothing at all mattered anymore.

"Stress can kill a cat." I've heard veterinarians say it again and again. I would have to deal with Clawed's mental state before I even began to tackle his physical problems and the first order of business would be a Snug Retreat.

Sacrificing one of my storage boxes, a nice sturdy Schweppes carton, I emptied the summer blouses out of it onto the dresser. I'd have to get myself another carton tomorrow. I moved Clawed onto the sofa and, laying the box on its side, I slid it in under the desk up against the radiator. Pulling out one of the desk drawers, I clipped onto it a 75-watt grow light and directed the warmth right into the box. Then I got Old Clawed from the sofa and slid him into his Snug Retreat.

I would estimate that, in the weeks that followed, Clawed snoozed away about twenty-one out of every twenty-four hours in there. The Snug Retreat is a little bit of heaven on earth for an arthritic old cat with failing kidneys.

Priscilla, my lovely Blue Point Siamese, observed all this from her lofty perch atop the bookcase. At age fifteen she had achieved a fine philosophical detachment and was quite content to let sleeping cats lie. That night my own three furry purries slept as usual in the bed with me.

But the luscious warmth of the Snug Retreat drew my little Priscilla like a magnet. No Siamese can resist it for long, even if there is a large and strange cat sleeping inside. Before long Priscilla's perfect little gray body could frequently be seen lying next to Clawed's bony one. Priscilla's figure was exquisite, her coat shining and soft. I had to keep reminding myself, "They're the same age."

Priscilla had come to me when she was twelve. She was a petite, cobby little Blue Point Siamese—the old-fashioned type, not inbred. At that time she was moderately healthy despite a poor diet in her previous home. Now, after three years of work on my part, she looked more like a crown princess than a middle-aged queen. I wondered how much time I'd have to work on Clawed; I wondered if I'd have enough. Fifteen-year-olds are slower to improve than twelve-year-olds.

"Nature heals," I reminded myself, "if only we give her the tools to work with." And as an all-around tool for nursing care, you certainly can't beat the Snug Retreat. Besides providing a place where a cat can "get away from it all," the steady warmth reduces the number of calories a cat needs to burn just to maintain body heat. Also, the light waves in the grow light spectrum are closer to those of natural, or full spectrum, light.

I am convinced that many elderly animals become increasingly vulnerable to various fungi and skin parasites partly because they tend to lie in dark places seeking warmth and quiet. Back in the days when I was working in a veterinarian's office, I had become aware that parasites such as ringworm and mites were most often found on elderly and/or diseased animals. In fact, I came to regard parasites as a veritable lurking menace for the older cat. Clawed's low vitality made him a prime candidate for fungal infestations, and with four cats to care for now, as well as a burgeoning business to run, I definitely did not need a ringworm outbreak to make my life complete.

Years later, I improved on the Snug Retreat by following the advice of Dr. Richard Pitcairn, veterinary columnist for *Prevention* magazine. I installed a fluorescent Vita Light® under my desk. (See Appendix C for suppliers.) The Vita Light® is a full spectrum light because it gives all the light frequencies of sunlight. Since it's a cool light, I also used a regular 75-watt bulb for its warmth. I must insert a word of caution here: *Never* use a *sun lamp* on a cat, or any other animal, for that matter. Those ultraviolet rays are much too strong, and even a short exposure can cause blindness.

I went out on the bike every day, paying grooming calls around town. The snow gets cleared away pretty quickly in New York. The snowplows are poised and ready to sweep away the bulk of it in half a day. Then by sundown the traffic has done the rest. As long as there was no wind or ice, I would ride. I prefer to be out in the fresh air. Every night when I returned to the apartment, everyone would run to the door to greet me and sniff the cold and damp from my fingers and boots—everyone, that is, except Clawed.

Clawed was too deaf to hear the commotion we were making and too deep in dreams to smell the gust of fresh air I brought in with me, and so I would greet the others and then seek out Old Clawed in his Snug Retreat.

Since he was deaf, I would always announce myself by rapping my knuckles three times on the floor near his foot. That way I got his attention and alerted him to my presence before I actually touched him. I didn't want to startle his old nerves.

The freezing weather lasted into the next week, but luckily Clawed was in no further need of veterinary care. When Clawed first arrived he could barely make it to the litter box and back again. Eating was an effort. Everything was a big project for him, and after each project, he'd sleep and sleep—Nature's prescription for healing.

I had started Clawed on the high carbohydrate kidney diet (see Appendix A) and was slipping in the appropriate vitamins so that Nature would have as much ammunition to work with as possible.

He had to be force-fed for the first few days because he was so weak, but he was a cooperative patient, almost too cooperative. I kept wishing he would exhibit some show of will, but apparently he needed more time. So I just let his body absorb the new diet while he snoozed away that first month, and I waited for the signs that would tell me that Clawed's system was changing gears.

During his few waking hours I let him know again and again that we were glad he was with us. Old cats like Clawed need frequent demonstrations of love. I sometimes wonder if they feel they are somehow lacking in appeal because they can no longer amuse us with lively antics or impress us with their athletic leaps. Whatever the reason, many older cats withdraw into themselves; they don't overtly call for attention as once they did. So it's up to the kindly owner to be sensitive to this subtle change and to make the overture himself. I found that it was altogether too easy for me to forget to do this for Clawed because I was so busy and the old boy so withdrawn. He had been conditioned to believe that the only good cat was an inconspicuous cat. So the only way to be sure that I was fulfilling his need for more affection was to consciously incorporate it into some activity I was already doing. For example, when I was sitting at the desk answering telephone messages from my clients, I would reach down and give Clawed a little head stroke at the end of each conversation. If I was writing, I did this at the end of each page.

Old cats, like kittens, sleep very soundly. Sleeping like the dead was a perfect description of Clawed's slumber. More than once I gently tapped his box and stroked him to rouse him slightly, just so I could be sure he was still with us.

By the end of the second week, Clawed was eating on his own. He would pad over to the food dish, stumble to a halt, and sway dangerously on his weak legs as he gulped his meal. He ate as fast as possible so as to finish it off before he fell down. After witnessing this performance twice, I moved his bowl close to the wall where he discovered that a cat could lean for support and munch away at a more dignified tempo.

Getting in and out of the litter box was like climbing Mt. Everest for Clawed. But, once inside, he learned to use the old "lean against the wall" technique again. However, several times he didn't have the energy to make it out again, and I came upon him sleeping peacefully in a corner of the litter box, head propped up against the side. I scooped him up, held him and rocked him and nuzzled him and, every time, he would look up at me and give me that old squint of pleasure, and his purr would crescendo until I felt my own body vibrating with his. I found myself picking him up and rocking him quite a lot. That squint and that purr were my first signs that we had a chance for success. A cat who can purr like that is certainly not a cat who has given up on life.

After one month on the kidney-building diet, the urine began to have a smell again, evidence that the kidneys were beginning to function as the waste disposal organs they are. Now Clawed was able to make it in and out of the litter box by himself every time.

Going into the second month, I noticed that Clawed was staying awake more. He would prop his chin on those big floppy front paws and watch with benign pleasure while Purr and Florence pursued a rollicking game of soccer, his round copper eyes gazing in wonder as their dented Ping-Pong ball went bouncing crazily across the hardwood floor.

I decided that he was ready for a little exercise, so I began placing him on his feet after our cuddle sessions as opposed to laying him right down in the box. After a week I began increasing the distance he would have to walk to get back to his box until, finally, I had him trekking a good ten feet three times a day. Afterward, he'd flop himself down under the warm light and sleep like the dead for the next few hours. I had to walk the fine line between exercise and overexertion. I judged that three short sessions a day would be easier on an old body than one long one.

Massage gives physical contact and a demonstration of love that even a deaf or blind animal can appreciate and enjoy. Remembering Clawed's joyful response that first time I groomed him at the Quincys, I made my stroking down his back firmer and stronger, using Clawed's response to guide me in how much pressure to use.

It was the daily grooming ritual that was the first "family activity" in which Clawed was able to participate fully. Of course, a few alterations in the grooming ritual had to be made to tailor it especially for Clawed's needs. The older cat's skin is extremely delicate and lacks almost all of its youthful elasticity. Combing and brushing must be done with a lighter and slower hand, especially for a cat as thin and bony as Clawed was. For Purr, Florence, and Priscilla I used the small, slicker brush. But for Clawed I changed to a natural bristle hairbrush. I made each stroke quite slow to insure that I would never knock the brush accidentally against a protruding bone. Old cats are delicate.

My next step was to find out whether or not Clawed would be able to use his shoulder and back muscles again. I wanted him to begin reaching out with his front legs. So, after his cuddle sessions, instead of placing him lightly down on the floor, I began stopping him in mid-air with his feet just an inch or so above the floor. His instinctive reaction was to wiggle a tiny bit and stretch his front legs forward as he tried to complete the descent. "Bravo, Clawed!" I'd say, and lower him to a touchdown, front feet first. Clawed's body was beginning to function smoothly again; it was a safe bet that the alkalizing vegetables I was using in the food were doing away with some of the arthritic deposits.

Unfortunately, Clawed and I had only recently met. If I had known him for a few years, I would have had yet another very powerful tool at my disposal, the use of old established rituals.

I encourage owners of older cats to continue any ritual activity that they and their cat have enjoyed over the years. The game of "chase the rope" before meals or the morning snuggle and romp under the sheets takes on a new value in the declining years. These things give a cat a feeling of security and continuity, as well as providing beneficial exercise.

Here in New York I know many sedate elderly cats who take an evening stroll up and down the apartment house hallway. This decorous and gentle activity began originally when the cats were very young. In the old days it could have included a scamper pell-mell down the hall after a ball or a tussle in front of the elevators with a furry feline neighbor. I encourage owners to continue the ritual of the hallway stroll, most especially in the later years. It makes a cat feel young again. It gives him a reason to get up and out of that warm box, move about a bit, and get the circulation going.

Naturally, a few alterations will have to be made in any game or ritual as the cat ages. You will have to be clever, and make these changes in such a way that the cat will never suspect that he is deficient or lacking in any way. If the exercise involves a game of chasing and catching something, you will have to become very skillful at engineering the game so that your cat will still "win" as often as he did before. Do you remember when he was a youngster, how quick you had to be to keep the rope away from him or to keep him from catching the ball on the first bounce? Now you must pull the rope a bit slower. Don't let him win all the time—there should still be a bit of a challenge there, but do be sure that he wins, at the very least, every other time. After all, the experience of success has great psychological benefit. And be sure to praise his cleverness, his grace and quickness. Tell him you're proud of him and that you wish you were as skilled as he is. The latest scientific findings show that cats and dogs can "read" your thought concepts, so don't lie—be sincere in your praise.

Clawed's water dish and special litter box were right beside my desk and, because failing kidneys cause frequent drinking and copious urination, I cleaned his box four to six times a day. If I had to be out for several hours at a time, I left two litter boxes there for him to use.

The bladder and kidneys of any older cat are not

what they used to be, so, especially if your home includes stairs, it's wise to make the litter box more convenient than ever.

I must, in all fairness, give credit to my feline co-workers for the part they played in Clawed's eventual recovery. After all, they took him in and nurtured him just as much as I did, each in his or her own way.

Purr has always been my cat-in-chief. That first night he demonstrated his acceptance of Clawed by showing off and proclaiming his territories. The fact that he was communicating with Clawed at all sent a subliminal signal to my two females that Clawed was allowed to stay. Purr is innately generous.

For her part, Priscilla always displayed impeccable etiquette when she snuggled into the Snug Retreat; she would reach her nose close to Clawed's ear and breathe softly to announce her arrival. When Clawed opened his eyes or lifted his head she would then lick his forehead two or three times, begging permission to stay. After Clawed had given her his eye contact of welcome, she would then settle in with perfect grace, her soft warm little body snuggled up against Clawed's arthritic hip joints. Priscilla was a lady.

Florence was a wonderful diversion. She is such a ditsy little ding-a-ling that not even Old Clawed could take her seriously. But she was the one who ultimately made Clawed feel really at home, really a part of the family.

It happened one morning when spring was in the air. I wanted to get out the kitchen window screen and put it in so that all of us could enjoy the fresh air, and so I did, which delayed the morning feeding. Florence, feeling impatient, jumped up on the counter to cheer me on and, as usual, I gently but firmly shoved her off. She leaped for her landing spot but, unfortunately, this time Clawed's tail was lying across her touchdown point, and so Florence landed squarely on the tail.

Clawed yelled with surprise, startling Florence. She responded by hitting him in the head and Clawed countered with bared teeth and a hiss right in her face. Florence flounced off, declaring in loud Siamese cacophony how insulted she was.

And I, who witnessed the little spat, was beside myself with glee. No cat is truly part of a group until he has a little tiff with another group member about something. Clawed had finally expressed himself in no uncertain terms, and it was ding-a-ling Florence who gave him that opportunity. For me it was that longed-for signal that Clawed had definitely come out of retirement.

GINGER'S STORY

JAMES FRANCIS VAX

CRIS ARBO

CHAPTER SIX

GINGER'S STORY
When the Time Comes

W HEN a pet dies, the owner's sadness and sense of loss are always accompanied by feelings of guilt. I found this human reaction inevitable as I became involved, again and again, with owners experiencing the death of a pet. It didn't seem to matter that the guilt was undeserved. Regardless of the money spent or the time lavished on the beloved companion, when death came the guilt followed, as the night the day.

If a cat had received a lot of care and attention over a long period of time before death, the owner would say, "Oh, I've been so selfish to make her stay with me these last weeks. I should have let her go sooner." If a painful, fatal disease was diagnosed, and, at the suggestion of two or more veterinarians, a cat was put to sleep to avoid suffering, the owner would blame himself for not seeking yet another opinion or trying some experimental procedure.

169

It boiled down to either, "Maybe there was something else we should have done," or "Maybe we did too much." How can you help someone handle this guilt? All I do is let the owner know, repeatedly if necessary, that these feelings are not unique and not permanent. They will eventually pass.

I've also seen that the owners who carry the best memories for the rest of their lives are the ones who have carefully supervised the pet's last moments. Either they themselves were present to hold the animal and provide an atmosphere of calm reassurance, or they had appointed, in advance, a trusted friend of the pet to be there.

People are often amazed at the deep well of strength and calm they discover within themselves at that time. What I see is that special look of pride and love on an owner's face when he or she says, "She went so peacefully. I know. I was there with her the whole time."

In this situation most people would picture a very mature individual, someone of wide experience, and a cat who has shared a long life with that owner, through good times and bad from kittenhood to old age. But the cat whose passing I want to tell about was a different kind of cat altogether and her owner a special sort of person. They didn't fit into that category at all.

It was late on a rainy October afternoon when I locked my bike to the no-parking sign outside the old brownstone on East Fifty-ninth Street. I noticed that they were just taking the kittens out of the display window at the Humane Society down the street.

I mounted the front steps, rang the bell, and my new client buzzed me in. I started up the four flights of stairs with the heavy black grooming bag bouncing against my hip; rainwater was dripping on the carpeted stairs. My collar was wet, my cuffs were wet, and my socks were making squishy sounds inside my rubber boots.

I had put my dinner on hold to come pedaling pell-mell through the rain and rush-hour traffic in response to a phone call from a young woman who begged me to come bathe a cat who, she assured me, was in imminent danger of poisoning herself. The cat, she said, was trying to lick off some heavy black stove grease which was "completely coating her entire body." The plea sounded exaggerated. Nevertheless, one mustn't take chances; I said I'd come.

As I puffed my way around the last turn of the stairs and started up to the fourth floor, the door above me opened and I saw a slim young girl standing there clutching to her bosom the filthiest, scruffiest-looking creature I had ever set eyes on. I assumed that was the cat.

"Oh, thank you so much for coming," she spoke in a rush. "I'm Nancy Gallagher. I just arrived from Ohio, and I moved in this afternoon, and I just didn't know *what* in the world to do."

I stood there nodding and catching my breath. The cat hadn't moved a muscle; the eyes were fixed straight ahead, staring at nothing.

The girl took a step backward into the room, gracefully avoiding an enormous carton just inside the door. The apartment was totally bare—no furniture, no rugs, no curtains to cover the dirty French windows—only cartons all about. Several dozen of them were stacked on the low windowsill and against the wall. She continued talking quickly, as if she were afraid I might change my mind and go back home now that I had seen the actual condition of the cat.

"She came with the apartment," she said. "Someone just left her here, all alone. Can you imagine?" Her brown eyes were wide with incredulous horror.

I kept on nodding and dripping, catching my breath, and moved into the kitchen to begin unpacking my gear. Girl and cat followed close at my heels.

"I found her all huddled up like an old pile of rags behind that filthy stove."

Indeed, the grease and dirt from the filthy stove were very much in evidence all over Nancy Gallagher's cheek and chin and across the front of the formerly crisp white blouse, against which the underfed specimen was gently cowering. Nancy carefully disengaged the cat's claws from the sleeve of her blouse and lowered her onto the drainboard where she crouched in a tight little ball, still staring at nothing.

"I've been afraid to put her down," she sighed, "for fear she'd start to lick herself."

We groomed her there on the drainboard. Nancy was a very good assistant, petting and distracting the cat while I cut away the heaviest mats from her chest, abdomen, and outer thighs, where the stove grease mingling with dirt off the floor had done its worst. The cat lay still—too still, I thought, and I searched my memory for methods of dealing with an animal in shock.

In the warm bath, happily, I felt her stir and begin to relax. So did I, now that the delicate business of cutting out mats was behind me. While I bathed the cat and Nancy nuzzled and petted her, we talked. Nancy had just graduated from a small Midwestern college. She had recently accepted a very minor position with a major airline and was all agog at the prospect of "making her own life" in New York City. She was destined, in a few years, to climb to an executive position, but back then she was just a very new girl in the very big city.

The bath turned out to be a rousing success for all concerned—a new life experience for both Nancy and her new friend. Of course, all Nancy's nuzzling and petting resulted in the one ending up as soggy as the other by the time I pronounced the cat clean and called for one of the towels Nancy had warming in front of the stove.

After our skinny friend was finally dry and even fluffy in the places where she had any hair left, she further calmed our concern by polishing off a modest supper. The danger of shock was definitely past.

We sat down with a nice hot cup of tea, and I watched the little cat nibbling daintily, engrossed in the very important business of eating. "Look at that fur shine!" I was proud of my handiwork. "You can see she's actually quite red, and I'll bet her hair is going to be rather long, once it grows in. I think you have yourself a Maine coon cat there."

"She's a ginger cat," Nancy responded, "Ginger." The cat looked up from her dish at Nancy and their eyes met. "I'll call you Ginger."

And a very contented, very clean and relaxed pussycat came trotting across the floor, leaped up onto Nancy's lap, and settled herself there in a neat little heap. She looked over to where I was sitting and sent me one slow blink of contentment before she tucked her nose under her tail and dropped off to sleep.

It wasn't two weeks later when I found a message from Nancy on my answering machine. Calm and succinct, she asked if I would stop by at my earliest convenience, any day after five-thirty. More grease, I wondered? It didn't sound like it.

This time, when I arrived, tea was served at once. I looked around me with pleasure. The walls had been painted white. The only furniture was a white wicker set of sofa, chair, and coffee table—secondhand, she told me, from the thrift shop near First Avenue. The old oak floors had been waxed, and filmy white curtains framed the big French windows, which had been fitted with screens. The plants that ran riot in and around the windows were "treasures from the trash," as Nancy put it. They had all been snatched, quite literally, from the very jaws of the garbage disposal truck, then lugged, battered and bedraggled, up the four flights of stairs, and deposited in Nancy's sunny window where they now thrived in what looked to me to be plant heaven.

A late afternoon sun was streaming in past the plants and fell on a small red throw rug where Ginger lay stretched out on her side, idly nibbling the rough edge off a dewclaw. She looked content and happy, but I noticed that now, two weeks after her bath, her coat was already dull and she hadn't begun to flesh out as I'd expected.

Nancy's news wasn't good. As I had suggested, she had let Ginger settle in for a week while she fed her my Basic Diet III—the homemade food (see Appendix

A, page 200). Then she made an appointment at the Humane Society's clinic for a thorough exam and teeth cleaning. The exam had been done. The teeth cleaning had not.

"She's dying, Anitra." It was a quiet statement of defeat. "She was left here all alone to die. The veterinarian says she's at least twelve or fourteen years old, and she has a great big tumor in her chest. She tries to play, but she gets all out of breath because she can't breathe right and sometimes she can't even swallow right."

There it was. I wondered why Nancy called me here, why she'd brought Ginger back home again instead of simply having her put to sleep. I soon found out.

"I want her to have a last few days of happiness," she said. Her words came rushing again, "Just to be warm and safe and fed . . . just to be allowed to go at her own pace. I mean, after all she's been through . . . well, there must be something we can do." She looked at me, her brown eyes pleading, afraid I wouldn't understand.

I understood.

If Nancy wanted to go the limit for her little foundling, there certainly was plenty we could do. The first step was a second opinion. Whenever a major illness is diagnosed, or major surgery is suggested, or, certainly, whenever euthanasia (putting an animal to sleep) is being considered, a second opinion will be helpful to the veterinarian and reassuring to the owner. Even when the diagnosis is confirmed, alternative or additional treatment can sometimes be suggested.

I sent Nancy and Ginger to Dr. McAlister, who was

accustomed to my "interesting" cases by now. She confirmed the first diagnosis and pointed out that an emergency measure was necessary if we expected to shrink the tumor before it pressed the esophagus closed and choked the cat. She suggested cortisone therapy.

It worked. In one day Ginger was breathing more easily, and the doctor ventured a guess that we could expect the patient to live several weeks or maybe even two or three months. Eventually, of course, the cortisone would cease to have an effect. Cortisone isn't a cure, it's a stop-gap measure and we knew it, but it was the best that anyone could do in those days.

During the following week I talked with the doctor over the phone. I got her okay to try to slowly substitute a special homeopathic preparation of goldenseal herb for part of the cortisone dose. I was hoping to stretch out the length of time the cortisone would be effective. We were successful. Over the course of three weeks we had substituted the herbal preparation for two-thirds of the cortisone. Then the doctor advised us not to push our luck any further.

Nancy kept Ginger on Basic Diet III, including the alkalizing vegetables—carrot, celery, string beans, zucchini, or alfalfa sprouts. She also began to supplement the diet with additional vitamins A, C, and E and mixed minerals to minimize the side effects of the cortisone. Dr. McAlister gave her okay. "It certainly can't hurt," she said. And with Nancy's attention, Ginger outlived all the doctor's predictions and kept Nancy company for three years.

Nancy had scheduled monthly groomings, so, over the next three years, I had the pleasure of watching skinny, weak Ginger blossom into a strong, calm, lush-coated beauty. Her comic antics and *joie de vivre* were exceeded only by her boundless love for Nancy, her darling human pet, whom she seemed to cherish as something between a recalcitrant kitten and a favorite slave—roles Nancy filled with great tenderness and love. At the end of the grooming there was always the nice hot cup of tea while we congratulated each other on Ginger's condition.

The object of our discussions would sprawl on her little red rug, daintily nibbling her freshly manicured claws into the shape dictated by her own fastidious tastes. A grooming and massage by Anitra were very nice indeed, but from a cat's point of view, when it comes to the finishing touches, there's nothing quite like one's own teeth and tongue.

Nancy placed her cup and saucer on the coffee table and leaned back, as relaxed as Ginger. "I certainly got my wish," she smiled, "she's the picture of innocent bliss. She has no idea that anything is wrong with her."

"To a cat, the present is really the only time that has relevance," I said. "Lessons learned in the past will influence present behavior, but the past itself is forever gone, and the future, beyond the next few minutes, doesn't exist at all for a cat. Dr. McAlister puts it this way: 'Cats don't know what death is; the concept is foreign to them; so they don't know they're going to die.' We can use that fact to make things easier on them. Cats take their emotional tone from their owners, from the ones they love. If you can stay calm and happy, she'll stay calm and happy, right up to the end, unless there is some pain."

"Well, there isn't going to be any pain, Anitra, I've made up my mind about that." Nancy drained her cup and leaned back. "I've been doing a lot of thinking lately, and I've made up my mind on two basic points. First, Ginger is not going to be allowed to suffer; and second, I want to be with her when she's put to sleep."

I felt a flood of relief. Without any help from me, Nancy had arrived at a central core of truth. She had realized, as so many owners realize, that her own happiness and peace of mind were inextricably bound up with the welfare and happiness of her pet. What was best for Ginger would automatically be best for Nancy. How beautifully simple and clear the logic is when one thinks it through.

"You're right," I said. "Or, at least, you're doing what I would do—have done—many times in the past."

I went on, to reassure her and reinforce her decisions. "I don't think we'll have to worry about any actual pain. What we have to watch for is discomfort which could be frightening to her if that tumor starts to interfere with her oxygen flow. Call me anytime and leave a message on the answering machine. Meanwhile, I'll call the vet's office and advise her of your decision. She has twenty-four-hour service, you know, so we won't have to worry about not being able to get to her when we need her."

"And she won't tell me I can't be with her when she's put to sleep?" Nancy wanted to be absolutely sure.

"Don't worry, Nancy, you can be there. Remember, I've done this many times before. And I can be there, too. You can hold her, or I can hold her, and whatever happens, she'll feel nothing but love and quiet at the end."

Nancy seemed reassured; she could relax. And so could I—for Nancy, as far as I was concerned, was making the very best decision for Ginger and for herself as well.

Death, like birth, is a very important event for any creature, and it should be carefully prepared for, so that tranquility and calm will prevail. Since death is inevitable, it never ceases to amaze me that some owners refuse to face it. They are caught unaware and often make decisions on the spur of the moment which, later on, they sincerely regret, but must live with for the rest of their lives.

Euthanasia is a subject many people would prefer not to think about. But, if we wish to prevent a situation where, through ignorance or thoughtlessness, we condemn a loyal and beloved pet to spend its last hours or minutes in terror, loneliness, despair, or even pain, it is necessary to acquaint ourselves consciously with the facts.

Sick or dying pets are often simply dropped off at public animal shelters to be disposed of. The methods of disposal vary from individual injection, as at a veterinarian's clinic, to mass extermination, where varying numbers of terrified and hysterical animals are shoved into a small tank or compartment and slowly asphyxiated with lethal gas or suffocated by sucking all the air out of the chamber to create a vacuum. This last method has been outlawed in many states, but is still in common use in some areas. Even if individual injection is used in a public shelter, which is rare because of the time and expense involved, the animal spends its last hours alone and deserted, in a strange cage, and, at the end, is handled and killed by a total stranger.

I personally know owners who have left a dying pet at the local shelter to be killed. They did it because their families did it when they were children or because a neighbor did it that way last year. They followed this example because they wanted to do the accepted thing but preferred not to think too much about it. So they took their animal, who had given eight or ten or fifteen years of love, loyalty, and devotion, left it at the shelter, and turned their backs and walked away. Then a month, or even years later, they were unexpectedly faced with the truth about what euthanasia procedures are at that particular shelter. These people live with the ensuing remorse for the rest of their lives. It does not go away; they will always remember.

In the interest of prevention, I set down these facts so that owners can make an informed decision. I was fortunate to learn about euthanasia for the first time from Dr. Paul Rowan when I was working at The Cat Practice. I found discussing the subject terribly upsetting, even when considering it in the abstract with no particular cat in mind. Then one morning Dr. Rowan explained it very simply; "I just put them to sleep, Anitra, the same way I do before surgery, except I give them an overdose and they never wake up."

Carole C. Wilbourn, the feline behaviorist, once told me, "I can always tell when it's time; they get a certain faraway look in their eyes, as if they just don't care anymore." The loving owner will aim at choosing a time before the suffering begins, yet not rushing the pet out of life before it feels ready to go. There is a delicate balance to be achieved.

It was autumn of Nancy and Ginger's third year together, and the weather became changeable. New

Yorkers began putting away their summer clothes and taking out their woolens, and discussing whether or not the landlord would turn on the heat at night. I began carrying a hat, scarf, and gloves with me on my rounds and was always glad that I had them by the time the sun went down.

Predictably, at the first hint of a fall breeze, Nancy installed a Snug Retreat for Ginger. Ginger herself led me to the bookcase in the bedroom to show off her new acquisition. A bright red Johnny Walker carton lay on its side by the radiator. Nancy was leaving nothing to chance, for a 75-watt grow light was clipped to the lowest bookshelf and directed into the front of the box. Ginger began demonstrating the softness of a very tattered Navy blue cardigan, with repeated kneadings and circlings as she prepared to lie down.

"It's sanitary, don't worry," Nancy assured me. "I throw it in the washer twice a week. Ginger really enjoys wool more than terry cloth."

"Yes, so I see." I pitched my voice to be heard over the loud purrs and scratching sounds issuing from the liquor box. "Well, as long as you don't mind throwing your wool sweater into the washer . . ."

"Oh, it's *old*," she said.

Well, if it wasn't before, it certainly was now, I thought, once Ginger had finished kneading it into submission.

I hated the thought of taking Ginger away from her warm box, but she did have to be groomed and manicured. I needn't have worried. By the time I changed into my smock and laid out the tools, Ginger was up on the drainboard waiting in happy anticipation for her monthly beauty treatment. As always, Nancy was poised by the sink, ready to play her part in the ritual.

As I groomed each area of the cat, Nancy would utter a little exclamation of delight at the beauty of that particular part of her friend. She would murmur appreciative phrases about the fur of the inner thighs or the length of Ginger's whiskers and ear tufts. It was always exactly the same every time and Ginger loved the litany of praise as much as she loved the grooming. From a cat's point of view, familiarity breeds contentment. Nancy had learned this and used it to turn much of Ginger's life into a series of beloved rituals.

I began stroking and kneading Ginger's body and limbs, exploring for any signs of weight loss or unusual local sensitivity.

"Doesn't she look wonderful!" Nancy's voice was a bit too bright today.

"She looks great," I said, and meant it. "You're doing a fantastic job. How's her appetite?"

"Ravenous." Nancy beamed.

"Stools?"

"Normal—once a day."

"Urine?"

"Okay."

I worked on in silence.

Her eyes were watching me anxiously. I knew that Nancy's vigilance was covering a carefully controlled undercurrent of fear, hidden away in a safe corner of her mind. Nancy would thus protect little Ginger from feeling her own negative emotions.

I finished the grooming, noting with relief that Ginger's skin and fur were clean and dandruff-free. There was no weight loss that I could feel, but the unusual length of her nails told another story. Long nails meant that Ginger was more sedentary of late. The tumor was beginning to interfere with her heart and breathing again. Should I mention this to Nancy?

Tea that afternoon was served with my favorite Scotch shortbread cookies.

"A celebration," said Nancy, too cheerily. She had recently been promoted to head her own department. She was "Miss Gallagher" now, with a secretary of her own and her name on the door. It didn't surprise me. Big companies generally know a good thing when they see it. If she handled challenges at work anything like the way she'd handled the challenge Ginger had presented, that airline was lucky to have her. We sat in silence, watching Ginger enjoying her sun spot on the little red rug.

Part of my job as groomer and "friend of the family" is to help keep the owner emotionally "safe." Even a clear-sighted, courageous individual like Nancy will feel more secure, knowing that others have had to think through the same problems and have reached the same conclusions as they.

I have come to the conclusion that there are as many philosophies and religions as there are human beings on this planet. In the final analysis, no one can tell anyone else what to believe or how to feel. Furthermore, I am probably the very last one who should make such an attempt, since my own beliefs and philosophies always seem to be in a never-ending state of flux. However, reminding owners of solid facts can be calming. Facing a problem—as it is—is far less damaging than avoiding the truth and brooding about terrible and unlikely possibilities. I decided that the time had come to share with Nancy, for whatever they were worth, my own experiences and feelings where the death of a pet was concerned.

One fact that we must all accept is this: pets do not live as long as we do. Sixteen to twenty-five years is their maximum life span, and nothing we can do is going to change that. So, knowing this, it takes a certain amount of courage to own a pet. Our Ginger was already an adult cat of indeterminate age when Nancy found her. Dr. McAlister had said she had to be at least twelve, but she judged her to be closer to fourteen. At that rate, Ginger would now be fifteen or seventeen years old.

Death itself gives us two elements to consider. First, it is inevitable; everything that lives, dies. Without death there would be no life. Now let us consider its desirability. Death is, after all, an unknown. No one has yet experienced it and then reported back. My own question is this: Why should we automatically *assume* that death is an *undesirable* state for the one who approaches it, something to be put off for as long as possible and at all costs? It might be a kind of graduation to a higher existence, or some sort of reward. So let us freely admit that our sorrow is really for ourselves, who remain behind. Assuredly, there is nothing wrong with that. We will naturally miss the departed friend. However, if it is a beloved pet's appointed time to go, we who love her should certainly be the last ones to stand in the way of her smooth passage.

It is hard to live with the knowledge that a beloved animal's life is soon to end. Sudden, unexpected death can be a terrible shock, but it is in some ways easier than knowing far in advance. However, advance warning is not without its compensations. It does give us time to plan, just as Nancy was doing.

Since our life cycle is longer than that of our animals, it seems obvious that the grand scheme of things was designed to give us the opportunity to supervise and, to a large extent, control their final departure from this world. We have the magic wand, as it were. We can arrange everything for them, so that the end of their lives will be without suffering, and filled with quiet approval and love.

Even thinking about death is frightening to many people. Perhaps fear of the unknown is the basis of the problem. But being present when the time comes is a unique and golden opportunity to give a heart-felt thank you and to repay that beloved family member in a very real and meaningful way, for all the unselfish love, loyalty, and devotion that he or she has lavished on us. However, not every owner is emotionally suited to be present at an animal's death. Remember, this is not the time nor the place for tears or any signs of distress. The person who holds the cat must be able to provide an atmosphere of calm, quiet, and approval. If that is achieved, no matter how it is achieved, your efforts have been successful. Sometimes I advise that the owner not go along at all. Different people have different strengths and weaknesses. The tranquility and comfort of the animal should be the only consideration at this time. Even if you are as sure as Nancy was that you want to be present, it is always wise to have a trusted friend or family member along with you who can step in at the last moment if it seems it would be better for your pet.

March was surprising us all that year with balmy weather and sunshine. The result, for me, was sudden, heavy shedding from all of New York's felines, and I went racing around town on my trusty Raleigh three-speed from dawn till after dusk—combing, clipping, bathing, and generally having a wonderful time.

I was home by ten-thirty on Wednesday night. I spent the next hour greeting and feeding my own furry purries, cleaning the litter boxes, and, finally, dishing out my own dinner—Chinese take-out—I sat down at the desk to eat while I played back the day's telephone messages. One was from Nancy: would I please stop by at my earliest convenience any day after five-thirty. Nancy was being controlled and efficient again, and I didn't like the sound of that at all.

From late February through early May "my earliest convenience" can sometimes be three to four weeks away. I checked my appointment book: five-thirty tomorrow I was grooming Chuli and Fillip Aparicio. No problem. Olga Aparicio was typical of most of my clients: she'd happily change her appointment four or five times, if it meant helping a pussycat in distress. All I needed to do was explain that there was a cat who needed me more than her own two robust little beauties. I had a gut feeling that Ginger needed me now.

At five-thirty the next day, I arrived at Nancy's and found Ginger lying on her side on the little red throw rug under the French window. The minute she saw me, she pulled herself into a sitting position. Then, panting, she braced herself with her forelegs, too winded from that little exertion to stand up. Her hair was dull and lank again, her eyes puzzled. I went over and picked her up, cradling the little body against my chest, and met Nancy's eyes.

"We saw Dr. McAlister yesterday morning." Nancy's voice was under tight control. "She says there's nothing more to be done."

I groomed and massaged Ginger on the drainboard because I always groomed and massaged her there. It was a short, light, make-believe little grooming, more of a fondling than anything else. But now was not the time to break a well-loved pattern. I channeled the emotions that I wanted Ginger to receive from me by murmuring small compliments and endearments. Nancy stood gripping the side of the sink, silent, unable to deliver her lines.

Ginger's breathing was shallow and difficult, and she was beginning to be upset by her inability to call upon her breath at will. Soon she would become frightened. Clearly the time had come.

We left the carry case open on Nancy's lap in the cab so she could stroke Ginger's head. She channeled feelings of approval and calm to her by murmuring casual compliments about what a good traveler Ginger was. Nancy had gained control of her emotions.

I had alerted Dr. McAlister and she was ready for us when we arrived. We were ushered directly into the rear examining room where Ginger was gently lifted onto the table. The doctor took one look at her and then looked at me, her eyebrows raised in silent question.

I nodded, "It's okay, we're ready."

Ginger was panting quietly. Her head lay cupped in Nancy's palm. Her whole attention was on her struggle to get enough air. Nancy was stroking the soft fur between her ears, and crooning, "Thank you, Ginger, thank you for taking such good care of me."

Ginger sighed one time and then lay perfectly still.

The injection had been given. The doctor turned and quietly left the room. I laid my hand on Ginger's chest, felt no heartbeat and turned to Nancy, "She's gone now."

Nancy nodded and I too left the room.

I found my way back to the waiting room feeling as if the universe had gone into slow motion and I was swimming through the atmosphere. The only animal in the waiting room was a large half-Collie, a young dog sitting quietly beside a tall blond man with very thick glasses, the kind that make the wearer's eyes look enormous. Still in a fog, my mind focused, as usual, on the animal. I remember thinking how nice it was to see such a young dog who could sit quietly without fidgeting—evidence of adequate exercise and a well balanced diet. I wondered what the owner was feeding him.

Just then man and dog stood up, came toward me, and the man grasped my hand.

"I'm Larry Prince, Nancy's friend from work," he said. "I've known about Ginger for a while now. When I called the apartment and got no answer, well, I knew she wouldn't have gone out and left Ginger all alone, so I called here. We came right over."

My mind was still in that slow motion universe. I suppose I must have looked rather blank.

"Is she all right?" he asked. "Nancy, I mean?" The blue eyes were peering down at me through the glasses.

Then, slowly, my mind drifted into the present. This was a friend of Nancy's. He was concerned.

"Yes," I said. "I mean, yes and no." I couldn't frame my words. "She's doing fine, as well as can be expected."

He leaned closer, his voice low, as one imparting classified information. "You know," he said, "Nancy Gallagher is a very extraordinary young woman." He went on, "I'm so glad that you could be with them."

The dog's tongue flicked out and in against his owner's hand. He whimpered a tiny question. The man's hand came to rest on the dog's head.

"Sit down, Duke," he said. Duke sat.

"We can take over now if you'd like. You look bushed. Or we can just hang around, or bow out, whatever you think is best."

Suddenly I was myself again—bone weary, but back to normal. I decided that I very much liked this tall man with the dog. His hand clasp had been firm, his face was earnest, and I liked the way that dog was looking up at him.

"Thank you for coming," I said. "I'm sure you're in much better shape to take over now than I am. If you could please remember just one thing . . ."

"Yes, of course, anything." He swayed forward again.

"If Nancy starts feeling guilty, just tell her it always happens to people at this time. Tell her I said that it has nothing to do with reality, and it will pass."

The following morning an exquisite bouquet of daisies and forget-me-nots arrived along with a thank-you note—from Nancy, of course, thoroughly thoughtful even now.

There was a fire at the Humane Society in May. From what I could gather, it was mostly a lot of smoke, but the animals all spent an uncomfortable day sitting in tiny cages and carry cases out on the pavement. It was hardest on the infirmary cases. Thank heavens it was May and not December.

Nancy called that night. I should have expected it. After all, she had to pass right by the Humane Society on her way home from work.

"Could you possibly come right over and help us, Anitra? We have a terrible emergency here."

"Help *us?*"

"Yes, we're all over at Larry's place. We just don't know what in the world to do!"

Larry's place was on Riverside Drive—a fifteen-minute bike ride on a balmy May evening. The apartment building turned out to be one of those huge luxury buildings built in the 1800s—an enormous antique, beautifully appointed and beautifully kept.

Nancy let me in and hurried me through to the kitchen. Larry, silent and grave, trailed along behind. There was an underlying scent of smoke in the air, and something else.

"Duke and Princess are in here," Nancy said. "Princess is the one who needs you."

The odor was coming from here. Dog and cat were together under the big sink. For a moment I caught my breath—I thought the cat was Ginger. Princess was a young red Maine coon lying on her side on a white towel in an enormous gray plastic pan. Both her front legs were in splints, her nose and mouth were a mass of partially healed scabs and her hind quarters were encrusted with excrement. The dog was sitting facing the pan, ears pricked forward, watching the cat.

Princess had been in the infirmary when the fire struck. She had been brought to the shelter two days earlier by some children who found her lying on the pavement. Both her front legs had multiple fractures;

all her front teeth had been knocked out, and she had a hairline fracture of the palate. She had obviously fallen from an unscreened window or off a balcony or fire escape. It's a yearly phenomenon in New York. Hundreds of cats fall every spring when people open their windows and forget to put in screens. Veterinarians call it the "high-rise syndrome."

When Nancy and Larry passed the Humane Society late in the day, the exhausted workers had reached the reluctant conclusion that, because of the fire, there was no possible way for them to care for this cat who could neither use the litter by herself nor eat on her own. By the end of that terrible day she was hungry, thirsty, and covered with filth. The kindest thing would be to put her to sleep; then Nancy and Larry came along.

Now the little cat was safe and would soon be clean and comfortable. Just then she began to scrabble with her hind paws against the side of the pan. Duke stood up, looked up at Larry and began to whine and nip at his sleeves. Larry just nodded to the dog, then stooped down and folded himself under the sink. He slid one enormous hand under the cat's chest and the other under her hip and raised her up out of the box. He stood up, holding the cat across his palms, and moved her into a position above the kitchen sink. There followed a few seconds of hushed silence while the cat wiggled and shrugged and Larry readjusted his supporting hands to her liking. Then, she urinated—right down the drain. Nancy beamed, Larry beamed, Duke wagged his tail, and I just stood there with my mouth open.

Larry spoke over his shoulder as he folded himself back down and lowered the cat into the box again.

"Duke always lets us know when she has to 'go,'

so once you and Nancy get her cleaned up, Anitra, we'll be able to keep her that way."

Sitting in the kitchen with Nancy an hour later, it was a little like *déjà vu*. Another bath, another clean, contented pussycat, but this one was only two years old and as strong as a horse.

Of course, she had to stay with Larry until she could walk so that Duke could keep a watch on her and Larry could lift her around with his big hands. Naturally, that meant that Nancy had to spend quite a bit of time there too . . . naturally.

While Larry and Duke went out for their evening run, Nancy and I talked—about Ginger, about Princess and the fire, and about Larry and Duke. It was then I remembered to ask, "By the way, Nancy, what does Larry feed that dog? That's some fine animal he's got there!"

Nancy looked surprised. "Why, Anitra, exactly what I fed Ginger, of course—your homemade diet."

I started to laugh as she went on. "Larry found Duke while he was running in the park. The poor dog was starving and scared and just shook and trembled, so Larry took him home and fed him. Then he took him to the vet. He had worms and fleas and something else, I think. Why are you laughing?"

I just shook my head.

She leaned forward, lowering her voice, "You know, Anitra, Larry Prince is a very extraordinary young man."

Right before Christmas I was not too surprised when I received a wedding invitation. The service was held in Larry's enormous living room. Princess was all healed by then, and Duke and I agreed that she looked almost as pretty as Nancy.

APPENDIX A
Diets, Special Diets & Supplements

THE most common mistake in feeding cats is leaving food available between meals. Perhaps this is because the manufacturers of cat foods encourage it. The truth is, it's not healthy.

Look at it from Nature's point of view. If your cat were out in the wild, would the mice lounge around all day under his nose? Of course not. When a cat smells food, his brain is triggered to slow the body's metabolism in order to prepare for digestion. That means that both blood flow and waste disposal action are slowed down. If the cat smells food all day—it doesn't matter whether he eats it or not—all of the organs, except the stomach, will be undersupplied with blood, and, consequently, those organs will age faster. The slow-down of waste disposal causes a backup and a buildup of toxic substances within the cat's body. The body will then try to get rid of these toxic substances any way it can—often by pushing the wastes out through the pores of the skin in the form of dandruff. Dandruff cannot be cured unless food is removed between meals. Other adverse effects of leaving food available all day are runny eyes, impacted anal glands, feline acne on the chin, dull coat, matting fur, finicky eater syndrome, obesity, and skinniness.

Cats should enjoy their meals, and mealtimes should be joyous occasions. Don't dull the appetite and spoil the fun by leaving food around for them to smell all day long. Remember, an empty, dirty food bowl is just as bad, since the smell persists.

Feed your cat morning and evening, leaving the food available for half an hour, or an hour at the most. If your cat leaves some food in the morning, don't worry. *Take it away just the same.* Remember, you'll be feeding him again that night. I guarantee that your cat will not eat the same amount every day of the year. Anything between a teaspoonful and three-quarters of a cup is normal. After all, cats in the wild eat once a day and then only if it's a lucky day. By those standards, twice-a-day feeding approaches decadent luxury.

Your cat's meal should include not only protein, carbohydrates, vitamins, and minerals, but also pleasure, for both the cat and you. Certainly the meal must taste delicious to the cat, but it is equally important that you, the owner, feel satisfied with what you are offering. Tearing open a packet, reaching for a box, or opening a can and plopping the contents into a dish may be fast and easy, but it is far from satisfying to a loving owner once he or she realizes that none of the foods in these containers will fulfill all of a cat's needs.

Even if you use one of the commercial products that are supposed to meet "complete nutrition" requirements, the element of *freshness* is not present, the vitamin balance is frequently off, and many trace minerals are missing. Be aware that the written word is very powerful. When most people see a container marked "cat food," they tend to automatically accept that this is what one should feed a cat. In reality, no cat can maintain maximum health if all he eats is processed foods. Owners in general are becoming more aware of this, and many feel a nagging doubt as they open these commercial preparations. Dr. Richard Pitcairn, in his book *Dr. Pitcairn's Complete Guide to Natural Health for Dogs and Cats* (Rodale Press, 1982), explains the shortcomings and very real dangers of serving commercial pet foods with their highly questionable ingredients.

There are three types of foods I avoid completely. They are dry food (which does *not* clean the teeth and is very high in ash), semi-moist food (which has up to five different chemicals in it and a high percentage of *sugar),* and fish, especially tuna (because it contains insoluble mineral salts which can cause bladder stones and gravel). If you decide to use a commercial canned food (containing *no fish*) as part of your cat's diet, you can supplement that food with some of the missing elements—once you are aware of what those elements are.

The first is *freshness*. Living in a natural state, the cat would eat nothing but food that was alive just one second before it was eaten. The Kirlian experiments carried out in both the U.S.S.R. and here have used special light waves to photograph the vital life force in living organisms which is gradually lost when the organism dies. Obviously this vital force is no longer present in a container on the grocery store shelf or even in our own cooked table food. To replace this vital force, you can add a raw egg yolk three times a week and a teaspoon of finely grated raw carrots, chopped alfalfa sprouts, or fresh chopped chives once a day to the cat's food.

Second, to be sure that all of the vitamins and minerals are present and, most importantly, in a form that is easily assimilated by the cat's body, I have developed a supplement which anyone can make called the Vita-Mineral Mix. It supplies not only those vitamins destroyed by heat in any canning or packaging process, but also all of the trace minerals, all of the water-soluble vitamins, and vital roughage. Roughage is badly undersupplied in any processed food and is needed to keep the intestines functioning properly. The mix also contains a generous amount of lecithin for skin and coat beauty.

Because the Vita-Mineral Mix does not contain the oil-soluble vitamins A, D, and E, three times a week give your cat one-half teaspoon of cod liver oil and 50 units of vitamin E (one-half of a 100-unit vitamin E capsule). A commercial oil supplement for pets from the health food store containing vitamins A, D, and E can be used instead. Or, if your cat dislikes cod liver oil, you can substitute the contents of a vitamin A and D capsule (10,000 units vitamin A and 400 units D) given only once a week.

THREE NECESSARY ADDITIONS TO WHATEVER YOU FEED

1. Vita-Mineral Mix (Water Soluble Vitamins)

1½ cups yeast powder (any food yeast: brewer's, tarula, or flaked)
¼ cup kelp powder or granules
1 cup lecithin granules
2 cups bran
¼ cup bone meal or calcium lactate

Mix in large bowl and store in a covered coffee can or similar container. *Be sure to refrigerate.* All of these ingredients are available at health food stores.

2. Oil Soluble Vitamins

Cod liver oil (unflavored)
Vitamin E capsules
  or
Commercial oil supplement for pets containing Vitamins A, D, and E

3. Something Fresh

Raw carrot, finely grated
  or
Alfalfa sprouts, finely chopped *or* chives

THREE BASIC DIETS

Basic Diet I—Canned Food Recipe

Read the ingredients on the label of canned cat foods and choose a brand which has *no* tuna or other *fish*, no preservatives, and no by-products of meat or poultry. Pet foods containing these harmful ingredients are found *even on the shelves of health food stores*, so be sure to read the label carefully before buying. Some areas have pet food distributors who sell cat food by the case, which may save you some money.

In a bowl, mix together:
  1 can of food (approximately 6 oz.)*;
  3 teaspoons Vita-Mineral Mix
  ¼ cup water, to desired consistency (Ask your cat.)
  If you buy larger cans, adjust ingredient pro-portions accordingly.
Store the mixture in a jar in the refrigerator. Never keep the food in a can. This recipe makes approximately 3 servings of ⅓ to ½ cup each. To warm the refrigerated food before serving, put the portion in a mug and place it in a bowl of hot water for two or three minutes.

Before serving each meal, add:
  ½ teaspoon chopped alfalfa sprouts, chives, or grated raw carrot.
Three times a week, add:
  ½ teaspoon cod liver oil (unflavored) or one cod liver oil capsule administered as a pill (see page 216).

½ capsule (approximately 50 units) from a 100-unit vitamin E capsule.

or

½ teaspoon oil supplement for pets from health food store (be sure it contains vitamins, A, D, and E).

Basic Diet II—Baby Food Recipe

In a bowl, mix together:
- 1 jar baby food meat (any meat except pork, veal or ham)
- 2 teaspoons baby food vegetables (any vegetables)
- 3 teaspoons baby food barley or oatmeal (comes in a box)
- 2 teaspoons Vita-Mineral Mix
- 3 teaspoons water, to desired consistency (Ask your cat.)

Store this mixture in a jar in the refrigerator. This recipe makes approximately two servings. To take the chill off refrigerated food, put the food in a mug and set the mug in a bowl of hot water for two or three minutes.

Before serving each meal, add:
- ¼ teaspoon finely chopped alfalfa sprouts, chives, or grated raw carrot.

Three times a week add:
- ½ teaspoon cod liver oil (unflavored) or one cod liver oil capsule administered as a pill (see page 216).

½ capsule (approximately 50 units) from a 100-unit vitamin E capsule.

or

daily add:

½ teaspoon oil supplement for pets from health food store (be sure it contains vitamins A, D, and E).

Basic Diet III—Homemade Food
This is the very best diet.

Puree in a blender or food processor:

4 to 6 parts lightly cooked meat

Choose from: chicken, turkey, beef, lamb. (No pork, ham, or veal.)

1 part steamed vegetables

Choose from: carrots, zucchini, string beans, peas, broccoli, asparagus, yellow squash, sweet corn

1 part carbohydrate

Choose from: cooked white potato, yam or sweet potato; raw oat flakes (soaked in water for 48 hours); cooked oatmeal, Wheatena, Instant Ralston, kasha, baby food oats or barley

Liquid as needed for processing. Use vegetable or meat broth or water.

Store food in meal-sized portions (⅓ to ½ cup) in Zip-lock plastic bags in the freezer. Before serving, drop the plastic bag into a bowl of hot water until food is thawed. Before serving each meal, add:

1 teaspoon Vita-Mineral Mix

½ teaspoon chopped alfalfa sprouts, chives, or grated raw carrot.

Three times a week, add:
> ½ teaspoon cod liver oil (unflavored) or one cod liver oil capsule administered as a pill (see page 216).
>
> ½ capsule (approximately 50 units) from a 100-unit vitamin E capsule.

or

daily add:
> ½ teaspoon oil supplement for pets from a health food store (be sure it contains vitamins A, D, and E).

Finicky Eater Syndrome

The Finicky Eater Syndrome is a failure of the cat's normal appetite, causing her to either refuse all foods except one or two or to pick at the food, no matter what is offered, never eating a normal-sized meal. Such cats can never achieve even normal good health because their diet is incomplete, unvaried, and does not contain any supplements. The Finicky Eater Syndrome can be caused in three ways: allowing the cat to eat only one type or brand of food (a mono diet); leaving any sort of food available between meals; or giving frequent snacks. Here is how each of these feeding patterns affects the cat.

Feeding a mono diet (one food only): In Nature, cats are forced to eat a varied diet. They do not hunt until they are hungry, and they frequently do not have luck until they are very hungry, so they take what they can get. Mother Nature's menu abounds with variety. At the same time, we know that cats adore sameness; familiarity breeds contentment. When a cat expresses a preference for a certain food, an indulgent and well-meaning owner will frequently begin feeding that food very often. It's very satisfying to an owner to see a cat eat heartily. If the owner feeds the favorite food so frequently that the cat can easily fast between servings, the cat will probably do just that. Cats frequently fast in the wild—in fact, a short fast is very beneficial (read on for Fasting). However, the uninformed owner may become unduly alarmed by the cat's lack of appetite and will produce the favorite food even more frequently in an effort to tempt the pet. He will probably succeed, for now at least. The cat loves eating the same familiar food and the same familiar texture, to the point where he begins to think of that food as the *only* food—nothing else is edible. *Voilà*, you have created Finicky Eater, Type A.

Leaving food available between meals: In the wild, cats don't always catch prey, so Mother Nature must be certain that when they finally succeed, their digestive systems extract every bit of good from the food they do catch. Nature has arranged that the smell of food will trigger the brain center to prepare the body for digestion. Saliva and digestive juices increase, and the metabolism slows down so the blood supply can go to the digestive organs. It is the *smell* of food—not the taste—that triggers the brain. If food (or even an unwashed bowl) is left available between meals, that trigger in the brain will be activated every time a vagrant breeze wafts the odor to the cat's nose. Soon the trigger will wear out, and the cat will begin to develop indigestion from faulty processing of food because the digestive juices have been used up on false alarms. Instead of whetting the cat's appetite, the smell of food will make the cat feel ill and unsettled, completely destroying what little appetite he might have had left. Increasingly specific dishes will be required to tempt him to eat—exact temperature and exact texture, as well as exact flavor. In this case, the owner usually does exactly the opposite of what he should do; he leaves the food down for longer periods of time and in larger quantities, or tries leaving a greater variety available. Of course, this only makes the problem worse. The cats frequently pace and cry, demanding food while the bowls are full. When fresh food is offered, they take a lick or two and walk away. *Voilà,* Finicky Eater, Type B—starving in the midst of plenty.

Giving frequent snacks: This problem is not as serious. It works the way leaving food available between meals does. I am not against occasional treats, as long as the owner is not inadvertently encouraging the "food is love" syndrome. If the owner utilizes non-food treats as well as food treats and gives food treats no more than once a day (less often is better), then no harm is done. Remember, a treat is much more exciting and pleasurable if it is rare.

How do you know if your cat is ill or simply a finicky eater? Here are the finicky eater's symptoms:
- Refusing all foods but one
- Eating tiny amounts and walking away to return later for another tiny amount
- Dull coat and/or dandruff
- Lethargy
- Crying for food between meals

Here's what to do if you have a finicky eater:

- Let your veterinarian make sure the problem is not caused by a physical problem (e.g. dirty teeth).
- Institute Basic Diet I, II, or III, being sure to include Vita-Mineral Mix, which contains appetite-stimulating B vitamins.
- Feed morning and evening *only*. Remove *all* food between meals, but always leave water available.
- Stop all between-meal snacks until appetite returns to normal.
- Serve only a teaspoon of food at first, so you can see if the cat eats even one lick (one lick means that the new diet is now considered edible). Then give more if more is asked for. Be patient.
- If not even one lick is taken, remove all food until the next meal. Then try another variation of the diet—perhaps a different vegetable or meat.
- According to veterinarians, cats can fast for five days. I recommend a slower, gentler approach. If the cat has not eaten *at all* after two days (four meals of not eating at all), mix the old diet with the new food half and half.
- Continue to decrease the ratio of old food. Do not feed a full meal until you have managed to lower the proportion of old food to nothing. You want to keep the cat's appetite sharp.
- When the new food is fully accepted:
  - *Never* feed the old food again.
  - Be sure to feed a variety of foods.
  - Keep snacks to less than one a day.
  - Never leave food or a dirty food bowl lying around between meals.

Alkalizing Vegetables and Herbs

A body with the proper acid/alkaline balance is resistant to germs, viruses, fungi, and parasites. Conversely, diseases such as diabetes, urinary problems, the cancers, most infections, and a host of skin problems will grow and thrive in an overly acidic body. In other words, most diseases are really symptoms of an acidic system.

The low-quality protein of dry food, the high sugar content of semi-moist foods, and the badly balanced all-meat diets all promote an acidic body condition and an alkaline urine. (The urine should be acidic.) Therefore, I frequently recommend including alkalizing vegetables in a cat's food or even administering an alkalizing herbal preparation in order to hasten the body's return to normal. The veterinarian should be consulted for treatment of any disease that has resulted from the acidic condition of the body. However, if the same poor diet causes the same old acidic condition to continue in the body, the same disease will probably return before long, or a worse one will take its place. So, while the veterinarian treats the disease, you can use foods to alkalize the cat's system and make it an inhospitable place for those attacking organisms.

Alkalizing vegetables:
Choose from these when making food for a sick or elderly cat: carrot, celery, zucchini, string beans, alfalfa sprouts.

Alkalizing herbs:
Garlic: Cats enjoy a pea-sized piece of garlic crushed and well mixed into the food three to

seven times a week. It lowers blood sugar and
has flea repelling and antibiotic properties.
Goldenseal (see page 210)
Ginseng: Ginseng is alkalizing and strengthening, and when used in a special ginseng-
royal jelly mixture (available from oriental
stores), it stimulates the appetite. Ginseng can
be purchased in extract or root form from health
food stores, pharmacies, and oriental groceries
and pharmacies. Make a tea using a few drops
of extract or by boiling a small piece of root. It
should taste slightly sweet. Give in doses of
four to six drops once or twice a day.

NOTE: When working to produce an alkaline condition
in the body, *avoid* feeding potato, tomato, and eggplant.
Although these foods can contribute to a normal healthy
cat's diet, they tend to produce an acidic condition and
should not be included if your objective is to alkalize
the system.

Fasting

NOTE: Fasting is *not* appropriate for cancer, diabetes, or
hypoglycemia patients, nor for pregnant or lactating females
nor for immature animals.

Fasting is a safe and gentle way of rapidly ridding
the body of a backup of old wastes. Since most diseases
result, at least in part, from a backup of wastes, animals
in the wild fast whenever they become ill. They do it
naturally, as a matter of course. When a pet becomes
ill and stops eating, I do not advise immediate force
feeding. On the contrary, for most skin problems, for

arthritis, cystitis, and almost any problem except diabetes, hypoglycemia, and cancer, a short fast of one or two days will work wonders, and there is no better or faster way to cure the Finicky Eater Syndrome. Many owners routinely fast their pets on the High Calcium Chicken Broth (read on for the receipe) once a week.

Fasting Method:
• Prepare High Calcium Chicken Broth (Recipe page 209).
• Allow animals all the broth they want morning and evening, but no solid food.
• Use no supplements.
• Provide fresh water all day—spring or distilled water is always best, especially during a fast.

Detoxification

Very few cats are lucky enough to be raised on a homemade diet, free of chemicals, hormones, and antibiotics. Besides these chemicals ingested with the food, many cats have been exposed to flea collars and powders, the fumes from room deodorizers, moth preparations, or car exhausts. Also many homes use commercial cleaning and germicide preparations which contain chemicals harmful to cats. These poisonous chemicals are all either stored in the body fat or deposited in joints or artery walls. If food is left available between meals, the general metabolism will be sluggish, resulting in a backlog of old body wastes clogging blood vessels and causing deposits to be formed in joints. Since all commercial food is low in bulk, or roughage, intestinal action will be weak, and intestinal walls will be coated with old fecal matter. Body pollution lowers resistance to all disease and makes a cat old before his time, but the condition is not irreversible. Becoming aware that an undesirable condition exists is the first step toward correcting it. The owner can then begin a detoxification program.

Detoxification is carried out in several ways: unclogging blood vessels and joints, cleaning the intestines, speeding up the metabolism (strengthening intestinal action and increasing blood flow), and, of course, eliminating all sources of poisons from the cat's environment.

Detoxification Program:

- Eliminate all sources of pollution (as given above).
- Feed twice a day and be sure to remove all food after a half-hour.
- Add to each meal:
  ¼ teaspoon bran (in addition to bran in Vita-Mineral Mix) *or* two presoaked wheat grass pellets
  ¼ teaspoon lecithin (in addition to lecithin in Vita-Mineral Mix)
  ¹⁄₁₆ teaspoon sodium ascorbate powder *or* 250 units vitamin C

- Continue to use the Vita-Mineral Mix in each meal as instructed in Basic Diets I, II, or III.
  (*Note:* Instead of adding extra bran and lecithin separately as given above, you can double the bran and lecithin in the Vita-Mineral Mix recipe and add 1½ teaspoons per meal instead of 1 teaspoon).
- Once a day, add to meal:
  2–3 mg. zinc
  Extra ½ teaspoon finely grated raw carrot

- 3 to 5 times a week, add to meal:
  1 very small clove of crushed raw garlic
- Fast on High Calcium Chicken Broth one day a
  week (see Fasting, and High Calcium Chicken
  Broth).

High Calcium Chicken Broth

The High Calcium Chicken Broth has many uses. Nourishing and easy to digest, it is excellent for the sick, nursing mothers, the very old, and the very young. Whenever a cat shows early symptoms of any illness, a one-day fast on this broth will rest the body, leaving more energy to fight off the disease. I and many of my clients have a "chicken soup day" once a week as a preventive measure. Serve the broth morning and evening and allow your cats to have all they want at these mealtimes (but no other food), taking up the leftover broth after a half-hour, as usual. Sometimes a cat who is ill will not eat the broth or will have only a sip or two. That's fine—just continue to present the broth on schedule. When the cat's body is ready to handle food again, the chicken broth is an ideal way to start.

To prepare High Calcium Chicken Broth:
  Chicken necks and backs (enough to fill large
    pot ¾ full)
  Green tops from one bunch of carrots
  1 teaspoon fresh lemon juice

  Put chicken necks and backs and carrot tops in large pot and fill to within one inch of the top with water. Simmer 2 to 3 hours, adding liquid as needed. It should just cover the chicken bones. Pour off broth and save. Add more water, enough to *barely* cover bones. Add lemon juice. (The calcium in the bones will dissolve in the acid from the lemon juice.) Simmer another half hour; the broth will look whitish. Drain off liquid and store with first-stored liquid.

Goldenseal

Goldenseal is an herb which can be purchased in extract or powder form in health food stores and large pharmacies. It is extremely alkalizing and should be used sparingly and never full strength. Its other properties include reducing swelling and inflammation and discouraging fungus. Here are three ways to prepare goldenseal:

Elixir:
Into a dropper bottle mix:
10 drops brandy
18 drops distilled water
2 drops goldenseal extract
Shake vigorously *3 minutes* (hit bottle against mattress as you shake). Store in dark cool place. Give 2–4 drops in side of cat's mouth 2 hours after supper or before bed.

Eyewash:
To a teaspoon of optical saline solution (available in drug store) add: one drop goldenseal extract. To administer, saturate cotton ball and squeeze 2–3 drops into each eye. Refreshes and

helps open tear ducts that have been swollen shut.

Salve:

Mix ½ teaspoon goldenseal extract with ½ teaspoon of any olive oil or bee's wax-type salve (available in health food store). Rub on itching or swelling caused by insects or fungus.

Pregnancy and Lactation Supplements

When a female cat is pregnant and during the time she is nursing her young, her nutritional requirements skyrocket, especially for vitamins A, D, and E and calcium. You can meet these unusual requirements by altering the diet as follows:

- Feed the pregnant or nursing cat Basic Diet I, II, or III. Be sure to include Vita-Mineral Mix, fresh vegetables (especially alfalfa sprouts) and add ¼ teaspoon olive oil or butter to each meal.
- Prepare High Calcium Chicken Broth and add to each cup:
  2 teaspoons yeast powder and ¼ teaspoon butter
  Feed one cup of this soup once a day with other food.
- Once a day, give:
  50 units vitamin E (one-half of a 100-unit capsule); ¼ teaspoon cod liver oil *or* for six days of the week, give a 10,000 unit vitamin A capsule, and, on the seventh day, give a 10,000 unit vitamin A with 400-unit vitamin D capsule (vitamins A and D come together in one capsule, available at health food stores).

Special Supplements During Medication

When your veterinarian prescribes medication, be sure to ask what family the medication belongs to (i.e. antibiotic, diuretic, etc.). Then, armed with this information, you can supplement your cat's diet accordingly. All medications have side effects which you can cushion or even eliminate by giving extra nutritional supports at this time.

MEDICATION	*FOOD SUPPLEMENT*
Antibiotic (Always administer for the prescribed length of time— don't stop antibiotics early.)	No dairy foods. Add ½ to 1 teaspoon acidophilus (suspended in water, not lactose) to each meal while on medication and for two weeks after.
Diuretics	Add ⅛ teaspoon salt substitute (potassium chloride) to each meal. Add 1½ teaspoons Vita-Mineral Mix to each meal.
Steroids (Cortisone) (Taper dosage off gradually at the end as prescribed.)	Add 250 units vitamin C to each meal. Use a pill *or* ⅛ teaspoon sodium ascorbate powder. Add ½ teaspoon cod liver oil to diet every other day *or* 10,000 units vitamin A and 400 units vitamin D three times a week. (Note: vitamins A and D can be purchased together in one capsule.)

Mineral Oil (Such as hairball medications, laxatives.) Always give it more than two hours before or after meals— never close to food.	50 units vitamin E (one-half of punctured 100-unit capsule) *and* ½ teaspoon cod liver oil every day for one week.

Anesthetics or X-rays	100 units vitamin E a day for two days before and two days after and then 50 units three times a week as usual.
	250 units vitamin C with each meal. Use a pill *or* ⅛ teaspoon sodium ascorbate powder. Begin one week before and continue for one week after.
	Increase Vita-Mineral Mix to 1½ teaspoon with each meal.

APPENDIX B
Giving Medications and Nutritional Supplements

THE following is a variety of ways you can give medications and supplements. In every case the key to success is patience. Take one step at a time and try to make every step feel like petting. Move your hands slowly enough so that your cat will be able to feel what it is you're about to do, so he can cooperate with you. To condition the cat to be calm during the process, make it a habit three or four times a week to take the pill-giving position (see below) and just pet the cat. You will be teaching him that being in this position is just another way of exchanging love. Gradually, try to make him feel good all over by petting him all over, even the gums and between the pads of the paw. You will become more and more familiar with your cat's body and your little petting sessions will probably develop into a delightful massage for your furry friend.

Giving Pills

Step 1.   File down the finger nail on the index finger of your pill-giving hand.

Step 2.   Kneel down on the floor with feet together behind you.

Step 3.   Back the cat in between your legs and *tuck his tail comfortably around him.*

Step 4.   Moisten the tip of the pill or dip it in butter so it will slip down the throat easily.

Step 5.   Hold the pill between your thumb and index finger.

Step 6.   With the other hand, stroke the cat's head and mouth, then grasp the cat's face from above, with the thumb and index finger under the cheekbones (don't grab the mouth), and tilt the cat's head back *slightly.*

Step 7.   Open the cat's mouth with the middle finger of your pill-giving hand, pulling the lower jaw down.

Step 8.   Poke the pill way back down the throat, beyond the hump in the back of the tongue.

Step 9.   Release the cat's head and mouth.

Step 10. Stroke downward on the sides of the throat.

Step 11. Pet and praise the cat.

Note: **Don't hold the mouth shut.** A cat needs to open the mouth slightly in order to swallow.

Giving Paste or Gel Medications or Supplements

Step 1. Kneel down on floor with feet together behind you.

Step 2. Back the cat in between your legs and *tuck his tail comfortably around him.*

Step 3. Put a small amount of the paste or gel on your index finger.

Step 4. With the other hand, stroke the cat's head and mouth, then grasp the cat's face from above with the thumb and index finger under the cheekbones and tilt the cat's head back *slightly.*

Step 5. Open the cat's mouth with the middle finger of your pill-giving hand, pulling lower jaw down.

Step 6. Wipe off paste or gel on roof of mouth, towards *front,* just behind upper front teeth.

Step 7. Release the cat's head and mouth.

Step 8. Stroke downward on the sides of the throat.

Step 9. Pet and praise the cat.

Giving Liquid Medications or Supplements Using Dropper or Syringe

Step 1. Fill dropper or syringe with correct dosage and lay it on saucer close beside you.

Step 2. Kneel down on floor with feet together behind you.

Step 3. Back the cat in between your legs and *tuck his tail comfortably around him.*

Step 4. With the other hand, stroke the cat's head and mouth, then grasp the cat's face from above with the thumb and index finger under the cheekbones and tilt the cat's head back *slightly*.

Step 5. Insert dropper in side of mouth between cheek and teeth (into cheek pouch).

Step 6. Using 3 to 6 successive slow squirts (not all at once and not suddenly), empty medication or supplement into cheek pouch. Keep head tilted *slightly* back so liquid is allowed to run down throat but not too far back so the cat can't swallow. *Never* squirt liquid down the middle of the throat—this could cause the cat to choke.

Step 7. Release the cat's head and mouth.

Step 8. Pet and praise the cat.

Giving Eye Salve

NOTE: Because the cat usually tries to lick medication off the medicated eye, always medicate both eyes so the affected eye will get the benefit of the medication longer.

Step 1. File down finger nail on index finger of pill-giving hand.

Step 2. Kneel down on floor with feet together behind you.

Step 3. Back the cat in between your legs and *tuck his tail comfortably around him.*

Step 4. Put a dot of salve on your index finger.

Step 5. Stroke around eye until cat closes it.

Step 6. Place finger with salve just below the lower lid of the eye.

Step 7. With the other hand, pull the lid up, exposing eye and rotate salve finger inward, wiping salve off on the inside of the lower lid.

Step 8. Let go and praise and pet the cat.

Giving Eye Drops

NOTE: Because the cat usually tries to lick medication off the medicated eye, always medicate both eyes so the affected eye will get the benefit of the medication longer.

Step 1. Fill the dropper with medication and lay it on a saucer beside you.

Step 2. Kneel down on floor with feet together behind you.

Step 3. Back the cat in between your legs and *tuck his tail comfortably around him.*

Step 4. Stroke around eye until cat closes eye.

Step 5. When eye is closed, pick up dropper.

Step 6. Pull up lid with other hand.

Step 7. Drop liquid in eye near *inner* corner of eye.

Step 8. Let go and praise and pet the cat.

NOTE: Instead of a dropper, you can use a small cotton ball saturated with the liquid to be used. Hold the saturated cotton above the eye and point the index finger down toward the eye so that when you squeeze the cotton ball, a drop or two of the liquid will roll down the index finger and drop into the eye.

Giving Ear Drops

Step 1. Kneel down on floor with feet together behind you.

Step 2. Have the ear drops ready beside you.

Step 3. Back the cat in between your legs and *tuck his tail comfortably around him.*

Step 4. Grasp the ear low down on the wide part—never at the tip.

Step 5. Drop the correct amount of medication into the ear.

Step 6. Close the ear opening by pressing the back part of the ear forward over the hole and hold cat's head gently tilted so liquid can run down into ear. (Try to prevent head shaking.)

Step 7. Blot off excess medication with a tissue.

Step 8. Let go and allow cat to shake head.

Step 9. Pet and praise the cat.

APPENDIX C
Product Suppliers

THIS listing of suppliers is for the convenience of the reader. At the time of this writing, the companies listed supply one or more products that are acceptable within the guidelines of this book. This does not necessarily mean that the authors recommend *all* products made by these companies.

Product quality can change from year to year; companies can change management or policies or standards. Keeping this in mind, we urge you to be continuously alert and to *read labels* and product brochures carefully even for products you have been using for a long time.

There may be other very fine suppliers or new companies that are not listed here. Our not listing certain suppliers does not necessarily mean that we wouldn't recommend them if we knew about them.

PET FOODS/SUPPLEMENTS

Suppliers of canned cat food
Cornucopia, Veterinary Nutritional Associates, Ltd., 229 Wall Street, Huntington, NY 11743.

Optimum Feline Diet, Earth Elements Inc., P.O. Box 5249, Orange, CA 92667.

Suppliers of supplements and supplies
PetGuard, Inc., P.O. Box 728, Orange Park, FL 32073.

Suppliers of supplements.
Standard Process Labs, Inc., Milwaukee, WI 53201.

PET CARE PRODUCTS

Felix Company, 3623 Fremont Avenue, N., Seattle, Washington 98103. Suppliers of "Felix Katnip Tree" scratching post and Peppy Powder Kitty Snuff (catnip).

Herbal Animal, Box 8702, Oakland, California 94662. Suppliers of herbal flea products and other natural pet products.

PetGuard, Inc., P.O. Box 728, Orange Park, Florida 32073; Toll free # 800-874-3221. Suppliers of herbal flea products and other natural pet products.

Zampet Products, P.O. Box 12330, San Francisco, California 94112. Suppliers of natural pet products.

Armor Enterprises, Dept. CAC, P.O. Box 15411, Plantation, Florida 33318. Suppliers of full-spectrum fluorescent lights.

Duro-Test Corporation, 2321 Kennedy Blvd., North Bergen, New Jersey 07947. Suppliers of full-spectrum fluorescent lights.

HERBS, OILS, EXTRACTS & HOMEOPATHIC REMEDIES

Angelica's, 137 First Avenue, New York, New York 10003.

Aphrodisia, 282 Bleecker Street, New York, New York 10014.

John A. Borneman & Sons, Inc., Norwood, Delaware County, Pennsylvania 19074. Homeopathic manufacturing pharmacists.

Caswell-Massey Company, Ltd.—Address for mail orders: 111 Eighth Avenue, New York, New York 10011.

Laurie Daniels, 12721 Harbor Blvd., Garden Grove, California 92640.

Kiehl Pharmacy, Inc., 109 Third Avenue, New York, New York 10003.

Westwards Herb Products, 12021 Ventura Place, P.O. Box 1032, Studio City, California 91604.